W9-ATY-666

LIBRARY OF AMERICAN
INDIAN HISTORY

BEFORE
THE STORM

▲

*American Indians
Before the Europeans*

Allison Lassieur

Facts On File, Inc.

TO MOM, DAD, AND SUSANNE

▲

Before the Storm: American Indians Before the Europeans

Copyright © 1998 by Allison Lassieur

Facts On File, Inc.
11 Penn Plaza
New York NY 10001

Library of Congress Cataloging-in-Publication Data

Lassieur, Allison.
    Before the storm: American Indians before the Europeans / Allison
  Lassieur.
      p. cm.—(Library of American Indian history)
  Includes bibliographical references and index.
    Summary: A narrative history about the various Indian people of
North America and their way of life before contact with Europeans
  ISBN 0-8160-3651-9
    1. Indians of North America–Juvenile literature. [1. Indians of
North America.] I. Title. II. Series.
  E77.4.L37 1998
  970'.00497—dc21 97-50072

10/99

**970
LAS**

Facts On File books are available at special discounts when purchased in bulk quantities for businesses, associations, institutions or sales promotions. Please call our Special Sales Department in New York at 212/967-8800 or 800/322-8755.

You can find Facts On File on the World Wide Web at http://www.factsonfile.com

Text design by Robert Yaffe
Series cover design by Amy Beth Gonzalez
Cover design by Sholto Ainslie
Illustrations on pages 2, 23, 41, 63, 83, 103, and 121 by Dale Williams and
  Patricia Meschino

Printed in the United States of America.

MP FOF 10 9 8 7 6 5 4 3 2

This book is printed on acid-free paper.

CONTENTS

▲

ACKNOWLEDGMENTS

▲

There is no way I could have completed this book without the generous help of scholars, historians, and experts in American Indian archaeology from around the country. A huge thanks goes to Dr. Brian Butler at the Center for Archaeological Investigations at Southern Illinois University in Carbondale for being my main contact with the archaeological world and putting up with my incessant questions and requests. I'd especially like to thank the archaeologists who agreed to be interviewed and who maintained a good humor during the research phase of the book: Dr. Jerald Milanich, curator in archaeology at the Florida Museum of Natural History, Gainesville; Dr. Dean Snow at Penn State University in University Park; Dr. Robert Pearce, senior archaeologist of the London Museum of Archaeology in Ontario, Canada; Dr. Mark Mehrer, archaeologist at Northern Illinois University in De Kalb; Dr. Ned Hennenburger and Dr. Michael Fosha at the South Dakota Archaeological Research Center in Rapid City; Dr. Jeff Mauger at the Makah Cultural Research Center in Neah Bay, Washington; and Ken Shoenberg, archaeologist at the National Park Service in Anchorage, Alaska. I'd also like to thank artist Greg Blew for his beautiful archaeological drawings (done cheerfully on short notice), which appear on page 71.

INTRODUCTION

▲

Thursday, October 11, 1492
The moon, in its third quarter, rose in
the east shortly before midnight.
I estimate that we were making about 9
knots and had gone some 67½
miles between the beginning of night and
2 o'clock in the morning. Then at two
hours after midnight, the Pinta fired a
cannon, my prearranged signal for the
sighting of land.

Friday, October 12, 1492
At dawn we saw naked people. . . .

—from the log of Christopher Columbus

Most history books start here, the day an Italian sailor first sighted the land he later named the New World. But who were these naked people that Christopher Columbus saw on the bright sand of an island shore? Columbus doesn't tell us much about them. He wrote that they were an attractive people. They were friendly, had dogs as pets, slept in strange contraptions called hammocks stretched between two trees, and made beautiful boats. Columbus, believing he had landed in the Indies, called the

WHO HAS A RIGHT TO THE PAST?

For decades, Native American tribes have battled against the destruction of their ancestral sites. They have also worked to have returned to them sacred objects that were housed in museums around the country. In 1990, Congress passed a sweeping law cumbersomely named the Native American Graves Protection and Repatriation Act. According to the law, museums and universities were required to make lists of all the Native American objects in their collections. They gave these lists to any tribe that might be able to claim ownership of any of the objects. If a tribe requested that an object be returned, or "repatriated," the two groups were to work together to make the exchange as smoothly as possible.

One of the most important types of objects that many Native tribes wanted returned was the human remains and burial objects that some museums had. Many American Indian tribes believed that the spirits of the dead stayed with their bones. If the bones were kept locked in a box or behind a museum display case, the spirit was trapped inside with them. They believed that no matter how old the bones were, they had once been a living person and deserved to be returned to the earth.

Museums also had hundreds of sacred objects that Native American tribes had once used in religious ceremonies. Many of the objects are part of their cultural history, told of in stories and songs passed down through the generations.

At first, many archaeologists and museum curators were aghast at the idea of handing over priceless objects to Native tribes. They argued that the objects would not be cared for properly. Many tribes wanted to rebury the bones of their ancestors. If scientists weren't allowed to study these things, the thinking went, knowledge about the past would be lost. Scientists felt frustrated, and many became angry.

Many Native communities were upset, too. They considered these objects to be owned by the tribes. The bones were those of their direct ancestors. According to their beliefs and customs, they had a right to them. They weren't interested in having someone else study their history.

If an archaeological dig uncovered bones or other human remains, some tribes made demands that archaeologists felt were unnecessary and spiteful. Some American Indian tribes requested that studies being conducted on human remains be halted. There was a lot of anger on both sides.

Gradually, however, people calmed down. As museums and universities began working with Native people, both groups discovered that they had more in common than they had thought. Museum curators who feared that their Native American collections would be scattered found that not to be the case. Many American Indian tribes were satisfied to let the museums keep some objects and return others.

Today, representatives of various tribes work directly with museums and universities. They explain how to care for and store precious objects so that the Native beliefs can be honored. Since the law was enacted, hundreds of objects have been returned.

The law, however, did change how archaeologists work. College students are sometimes discouraged from becoming specialists in Native archaeology. Scientists in the field steer clear of dig sites that might reveal human remains, fearing that the sites could be shut down completely if they find anything from a burial.

But it has also done a lot of good. Archaeologists are much more sensitive to the beliefs of American Indians. They have a better understanding of how Native Americans view their world and their history. American Indian students who once viewed archaeology as suspect are being encouraged to become archaeologists. The hope is that the sites will work with their tribes to preserve and protect the objects that belong to them.

Although most people have managed to work things out, the debate rages on. Arguments and legal battles over the rights to objects continue to this day. It's certain that some knowledge that people might have gained from studying these objects will be lost to archaeology for good. Some of the information in this book came from the study of human remains that probably wouldn't be allowed today. Scientists may lose some historical facts, it's true. But they stand to gain new knowledge and a greater understanding of the cultures of the people whose past they all want to protect.

people "Indios." They were the Taino, a group of people who inhabited the Caribbean when Columbus landed.

The land that Columbus called the New World was not new, and the people he misnamed Indios were not Indians. It is estimated that, on the day Columbus sighted land, as many as 6 million people lived throughout North, Central, and South America.

When ancient Egyptians built grand pyramids for their pharaohs, powerful Native civilizations constructed elaborate earthen mounds to worship their gods and to bury their kings. While ancient Greeks and Romans created beautiful structures of white marble, people of the American Southwest carved breathtaking cities out of red sandstone cliffs. As shipbuilders hammered nails into the fragile vessels that took Columbus across the ocean, Native Americans designed and shaped wood into remarkable boats of their own. While Europeans struggled with disease, famine, and war, Native American civilizations thrived and grew.

Today archaeologists, biologists, linguists, historians, and others try to reconstruct the history left by these ancient peoples. Much of the time, archaeologists focus on the *material culture* of a people. These are objects that have been left behind: stone tools, bone jewelry, pottery, house remains, shell mounds, and other things made or owned by someone. These are the things that archaeologists dig up when they excavate a site. They look at what the objects are made of, when they were made, and where they were found. By putting the material culture in context, archaeologists can make pretty good guesses about what life was like for the people who used these items.

But this evidence tells only part of the story. Where the archaeological record is incomplete, scientists fill the holes with the *ethnographic evidence*—eyewitness accounts from early explorers, descriptions, drawings, legends, stories, and other information that describes events and people from the past. They also talk to American Indians living today, whose traditions and lifeways have been passed down through the centuries from their precontact ancestors.

The information in this book comes from both archaeology and ethnography, but it comes primarily from the material culture of the people who lived in North America immediately prior to European contact. Unfortunately, even the evidence that has been found doesn't cover all the tribes, clans, and peoples that lived during the time right before Christopher Columbus landed. There is so much that archaeologists don't know and have little hope of finding. In the East and Southeast, for example, the European invasion wiped out many tribes before anyone recorded their existence. Farmers unknowingly plowed the remains of entire villages into their fields.

The precontact Native American people who lived in some northwestern areas of the United States, including the Great Basin, the Plateau, and parts of California, remain a mystery to this day. Most of them were nomads, crisscrossing hundreds of miles of land as they followed the migrating buffalo herds. Archaeologists think that these people made small camps as they traveled, staying in one place for a few days or weeks before moving on. But they have no way of knowing where these camps were or where to start looking for them. When one is found by chance, it tells little of the people who made it. A few pottery shards, perhaps a charred buffalo bone or two, may be the only evidence that anyone had ever passed through.

In other areas, the effects of the Europeans were felt by native groups long before explorers ever set foot in their lands. Such things as disease and the arrival of the horse preceded them. Much of what historians know about these Native Americans is colored by this contact. It is difficult to know what aspects of their cultures were original and what was changed by this contact.

Because of this, this book focuses on those areas that are rich in both the material culture and the ethnographic record, giving archaeologists and historians a clear look into the daily lives of the people who lived there.

Also not covered in this book are the many beliefs and religions of the American Indians of precontact North America. Spirituality it played an integral role in every tribe in North America and influenced everything in its members' daily lives. But little in the archaeological record tells about the specific beliefs of a people. Those who study these groups can only make educated guesses based on the material culture. Early accounts from explorers are not much help because most Europeans perceived the people they encountered as pagans and heathens without religion at all. And today, many American Indians are sensitive to the portrayal of their religious practices and prefer to keep their beliefs private.

The chapters of this book follow the path of European invasion, from the first Spanish explorers who set foot on the Florida coast to the fur-clad English explorers of the chilly Arctic. Each chapter focuses on a specific area of North America and brings to life the people who lived there at a time before anyone had ever laid eyes on a white man.

More than 100 years ago, General George Armstrong Custer said, "We behold [the Indian] now on the verge of extinction . . . and soon he will be talked of as a noble race who once existed but have passed away." Fortunately, this prophecy didn't come to pass. It's true that many of the cultures that existed in North America on that fateful October day in 1492 no longer exist. But many more do, carrying the past into their 20th century lives through their legends and stories—and through the objects that their ancestors left behind.

NOTES

p. v   "Thursday, October 11, 1492 . . ." Christopher Columbus, quoted in Alvin M. Josephy Jr., ed., *America in 1492* (New York: Vintage Books, 1991), p. 13.

PEOPLE OF PARADISE LOST

PEOPLE OF FLORIDA

The year 1513 was a good one for the Spanish explorer Juan Ponce de León. That spring, he had sailed to the exciting New World, which Christopher Columbus had discovered only 21 years before. During the onboard celebration of Easter, called Pascua Florida (Feast of Flowers), one of his men sighted land. In honor of the day, Ponce de León generously named this "new" land Florida.

Ponce de León's legacy—as well as that of all the early Spanish explorers to Florida—consists of far more than the naming of an American state. Most of the original peoples of Florida no longer exist. They were wiped out less than 200 hundred years after the first European explorers came ashore. But a vast amount of evidence remains of their existence—thousands of archaeological sites, hundreds of shell mounds, and thousands of pages of 500-year-old documents describe the people who once lived there. This evidence provides many clues about how they lived.

The Timucua were a powerful group who occupied most of the northern third of the Florida peninsula from the Aucilla River east to the Atlantic Ocean and south almost to present-day Orlando. To the west, the Apalachee, lived throughout the Florida Panhandle and maintained close ties with the Timucua. The Calusa, another strong

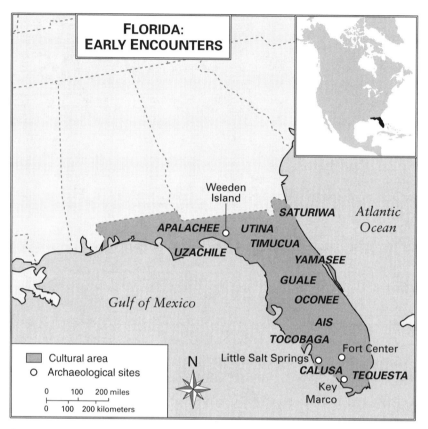

**FLORIDA:
EARLY ENCOUNTERS**

Weeden
Island

SATURIWA · *Atlantic
Ocean*

APALACHEE · UTINA

UZACHILE · TIMUCUA

YAMASEE

GUALE

Gulf of Mexico · OCONEE

AIS

TOCOBAGA

Fort Center

Little Salt Springs

CALUSA · TEQUESTA

Key
Marco

Cultural area
O   Archaeological sites

0   100   200 miles
0   100   200 kilometers

N

Some of the earliest European explorers came first to Florida. They found muggy swamplands along the coasts, but the interior areas were rich with farmlands and forests. The Florida peoples—especially the powerful Timucua—resisted the invasions but were eventually destroyed by European weapons and diseases.

group, lived in the southwest areas, making their homes both along the Gulf coastlines and in the wetlands of the Everglades.

To the north of the Calusa on the Gulf shores was the home of the Tocobaga. The Tequesta made their home near modern-day Miami. And there were many others that lived in Florida during the first wave of European exploration, from 1513 to 1539: the Yamasee, Guale, Oconee, Ais, and Chisca Pensacola, to name only a few. These tribes, like so many others in Florida, were quickly killed by disease, warfare, and slavery. Little is known of them but their names, and it's certain that others lived there of whom even less is known.

LAND

According to Dr. Jerald Milanich of the Florida Museum of Natural History, "In Florida, there were extreme variations. Roughly the northern third of the state was agricultural land. The people of the southern areas hunted and foraged." In terms of climate, Florida is almost like two different worlds. It was the same way before Europeans came. In the north, the weather is mild, with long summers and short, cool winters. In the south, muggy humid summer weather combines with a tropical winter climate that isn't very good for growing things. The north has forests; the central area has lands that are good for farming. But the southern and eastern areas have the most distinctive feature: water.

Until the last few decades of the 20th century, the entire southern tip of Florida was one huge swamp: the Everglades. This shallow but vast wetland once stretched all the way from the Atlantic Ocean to the Gulf of Mexico. Before contact, eastern Florida was full of rivers, lakes, streams, and tidal marshes. Along the eastern Atlantic coast, lagoons, estuaries, salt marshes, and freshwater wetlands teemed with fish, animals, birds, and other wildlife. In areas where there were large islands off the Florida coast, such as near present-day Cape Canaveral, enormous salt marshes and tidal streams lined the coastal areas. Surrounding these vast wetlands were dense forests that gave the Florida peoples almost everything they needed to survive: the animals and plants they used for food; wood for their homes, weapons, and art; and plants they wove into clothing and used for medicine.

On the western shores by the Gulf of Mexico, smaller marshes and swamps dotted the coastline. Inland, away from the ocean, fertile lands covered hundreds of acres. Here, Florida peoples grew vast crops of corn, beans, and squash.

PEOPLE

No one really knows for sure how many American Indians lived in Florida in 1513, when Ponce de León set foot on its sandy beaches. One estimate says that there might have been as many as 200,000 Timucua alone. As many as 16,000 Calusa may have lived near the Gulf Coast. Regardless of what the actual number might have been, it's clear that there were hundreds of thousands of people living here before European contact.

It was once believed that at the time of Columbus the Florida peninsula was home to two contrasting cultures: those of the north and of the south. Because of the huge variation of natural resources between the north and south, archaeologists once believed that the people in those areas had little to do with each other. It's true that the people of the northern areas relied on growing corn for food, while the southern groups relied more on hunting, fishing, and gathering for their existence. Archaeologists tend to classify a people by how they acquired food; farmers tend to live in one way, while hunter-gatherers usually live in another.

But the reality is that all the Florida peoples must have had close contact with one another, trading and traveling throughout the region. This undoubtedly enabled them to adopt one another's lifestyles, making their cultures alike in many ways. The vast network of waterways were perfect for travel, and dugout canoes were a major means of transportation for everyone. The natural landscape in Florida that enabled the tribes to interact so closely with one another is unique in North America.

The most powerful people in northern Florida were the Timucua. They included the Apalachee, who lived in the area near present Tallahassee, the Uzachilie, the Saturiwa, and the Uriutina. Although these tribes were separate and sometimes fought, they are known as Timucua because they all spoke a similar language. Their ancestors had lived in this area for thousands of years, from 11,000 B.C. The people who met the Spanish explorers are much more recent, though. In the book *America in 1492*, Dr. Dean Snow of Penn State University writes, "Archaeologists trace Timucuan culture in east and central Florida to about 500 B.C."

Archaeologist can see what some northern Florida people probably looked like from documents from early early Spanish explorations. The Europeans were fascinated by the appearance of the people they met and created drawings of what they saw. But their descriptions have to be read very carefully because they may contain European prejudices. The drawings of the people of Florida, especially the Timucua peoples, tend to be very stylized and somewhat unrealistic.

Many accounts accurately describe details of dress and appearance, however. "Numerous references provide at least some idea of what the Timucuans looked like," says Dr. Milanich in his book *The Timucua*. Men and women had a ruddy complexion, probably because they stayed tanned most of the year from living outdoors. Women were lighter than men, and they rubbed bear grease on their skin to protect it from the sun.

Both men and women wore their hair long, and men sometimes pulled their hair on top of their heads and entwined grasses or moss in it. Some Spanish accounts describe men sticking arrows in their hair, using it as a quiver. Both sexes had long, pointed fingernails that they used as weapons. Everyone had pierced ears, and decorative earrings included shell ear pins and inflated fish bladders.

Almost everyone had tattoos, and some specific designs were a symbol of rank. Chiefs and their families painted and tattooed themselves in azure (a shade of blue), red, and black. These tattoos weren't just small pictures but entire body designs, covering arms, legs, and even chests.

As might be expected in a hot, humid climate, the Florida peoples didn't wear much clothing. Spanish drawings show men wearing painted deerskin loincloths and sometimes loincloths of woven palm fronds. Women wove Spanish moss into short skirts. These were sometimes smoked over a fire, perhaps to make them insect-repellent. Chiefs or leaders had painted deerskin cloaks and painted bird plumes. The plumes were given away as symbols of friendship from one group to another and from person to person.

The Tocobaga, Uzita, Calusa, and Tequesta peoples lived in southern Florida. Archaeologists know that these people existed mainly from documents of the Ponce de León expedition in 1513, but very few details about them have survived. Disease, slavery, and warfare made these groups extinct almost before anyone had a chance to record their existence in any detail.

One of the groups, the Calusa, was perhaps the first North American people to come in contact with Europeans. Spanish documents, specifically the account of Ponce de León's 1513 explorations, mention a powerful Calusa chief named Calos. According to the records, he was the most powerful chief in south Florida. Most of the Spanish accounts of the Calusa focus on Calos's exploits, and little space is taken up with descriptions of the people. The documents do mention that many people had tattoos, painted their bodies with red ocher, and wore feathers and beads made of pearls and shells.

VILLAGES

People adapt their homes to their locations, and the people of Florida were no exception. The Timucua tribes in the northern areas had a climate and land suited to agriculture and took advantage of it. As Dr. Milanich explains, "Agriculture comes into north Florida at about A.D. 750. After that, for several hundred years, people scatter out across the landscape. We see sites all over the place, very small ones. Then, as they become agriculturalists, the populations grow. So then people begin banding together in villages."

Villages were built near the best land for crops and close to a freshwater source. An ideal place for a farming village was within a short distance of both fields and tidal waters so that the people could take advantage of the marine life there for food. When archaeologists look for a site, they usually look in places like this first.

Each family lived in a large, comfortable, oval-shaped house. These buildings could be up to 50 feet long and 40 feet wide, providing plenty of room for a family inside. "[They were] circular in shape, made of entire pines from which the limbs and bark had been removed, set up with their lower ends in the earth and tops all brought together above like a pavilion or like the ribs of a parasol," says Dr. Milanich. The houses were round because that shape tends to stand up to high winds and gales, which hit the Florida areas frequently.

The walls were made of thatch, wood, or, in some cases, wattle and daub. This is a mixture of mud and grasses that is molded into a claylike material and plastered onto a wall frame. Roofs were covered in palm fronds and thatch. Inside, around the walls, were low sleeping benches a few feet off the ground and supported by small poles. Hides and branches on the benches made comfortable beds. Underneath many of the beds were small smudge fires, lit to create smoke that would get rid of the horrendous mosquitoes that were a constant problem. Historical accounts mention these smudge fires, and archaeologists have found the remains of the fires in some excavated houses—right under the beds.

In the center of the house was a large shallow cooking hearth, which also heated the house in cold weather. Families hung food, baskets, clothing, blankets, and other personal belongings in the rafters above their heads. They also had baskets woven of grasses where they kept other belongings.

Outside the house, near the door, were usually other cooking pits, used for other tasks, such as smoking meat. Meat was placed on a wooden drying rack above the flames and left to smoke for a few days. Everyone stored most of their family's food in large circular pits outside. Many families also built granaries on stilts to store their corn and other grains. During harvest time, the granaries and storage pits would be filled with enough food to last through the winter.

Most of the garbage went into large pits dug immediately outside the village walls. Scientists consider a village garbage pit to be better than a treasure trove. Small bits of daily life that a group of people throw away can tell more about them than gold or jewels. Everything went into these pits: broken pottery and tools, the remains from countless thousands of meals, burnt food, discarded clothing and skins, the trash from making weapons and tools, wood chips from building dugout canoes, and anything else the villagers discarded.

Most Florida villages were surrounded by a palisade of thick wooden posts planted close together. These wooden fences rose up to 28 feet in the air and served as a defense against attacks from other tribes and, later, from the Spanish. All the villagers lived in houses built inside the palisade walls. *(New York Public Library)*

Small villages might have a few public buildings inside the palisade along with the houses. A large council house where people gathered for ceremonies and to socialize might be in the center of the village. There would also be storage buildings and corn cribs. Most villages also had a charnel house, a place where the bodies of the dead were prepared for burial.

Large villages, on the other hand, were built for comfort, style, and prestige. Some tribes in these northern areas lived in villages with thousands of inhabitants, governed by chiefs. These villages included many houses, council buildings, a chief's house, servants' quarters, and religious buildings. But their most impressive components were tall earthen mounds. The most important structures of the village were built on top of these mounds. These mounds usually appear only in the northernmost Florida villages, and they are part of the Moundbuilding culture of the southeastern and midwestern areas of North America (see chapter 3).

In the south, where the hunter-gatherer groups lived, large cities like the ones built by the northern farmers were rare. Because more time had to be devoted to getting and preparing food, there was less time to do other things, such as build cities or develop complex political structures. Southern tribes, such as the Calusa and Tequesta, lived in smaller villages connected by one leader or chief. Archaeologists usually find evidence of these villages situated along the coast or near wetlands and rivers. They probably held a few hundred people who made their living by fishing and hunting in and along the waterways.

Although no one has found the remains of a southern house, archaeologists think that some southern tribes had two kinds of houses: winter and summer. The winter houses, similar to those in the north, were round, with thatch walls and roofs. Dr. Milanich observes that "[winter] houses in the summer would have been very hot inside. They would really be for storage and for sleeping in bad weather." Summer houses were much more open, perhaps with lightweight walls made of palm fronds. These would provide shade but also keep the insects at bay. Underneath these houses, people built smudge fires to repel mosquitoes.

The most impressive site in many of these small villages wasn't buildings or earth mounds but enormous piles of discarded shells. These shell *middens,* as they were called, rose high in the air and consisted of millions of mussel, clam, whelk, and oyster shells that the villagers had feasted on and discarded over the life span of the village. Occasionally, the shells were used to build mounds, platforms, embankments, and walkways throughout the larger coastal villages.

In his book *Archaeology of Pre-Columbian Florida*, Dr. Milanich quotes an early description of the shell mounds. "Shell deposits . . . are of gigantic proportions. They are composed exclusively of marine species. . . . Anyone who for the first time views the larger ones sometimes covering several acres . . . rising to the height of fifteen, twenty, or twenty-five feet, might be well excused for doubting that such immense quantities of small shells could have been brought together by human labor."

SURPRISE AT A DIG SITE

In 1976, Dr. Jerald Milanich, archaeologist for the Florida
Museum of Natural History, began digging at a mound site in
northern Florida. He expected to find a chief's burial crypt.
What he found stunned him and changed how archaeologists
understand some aspects of precontact American Indian life.

"This was a site with three mounds around a plaza,"
Milanich says.

It turned out to be an elaborate charnel house where bodies
where prepared for burial. One mound was an area where
human bodies were cleaned and eviscerated. The cleaned
remains were taken to a charnel house on the second mound,
where they were stored. The third mound was the residence of
the woman who was in charge of the whole operation.

We know that they cleaned and prepared bodies on the first
mound by the kinds of bones we found there. You find little bits
that were lost or discarded—teeth, fingers, ribs. The only parts
of a body that were stored in the charnel house were the long
bones off the legs, sometimes other large parts, and the skulls.
These were bundled and stored.

We found pits where they had been burying people, then
exhuming them. Around this area, they'd built a big post wall,
because we found a wall trench where the posts had been. The

Based on all the evidence, archaeologists can make good
guesses as to how the Florida peoples might have gone about
their day. People of the southern areas of Florida spent most of
their time working outdoors. Some made nets and fishing tools
such as hooks, net weights, and spears. Others spun moss and
grasses into strong fibers for nets and clothing. On any given
day, canoe builders might have been near the shore, repairing
canoes or carving paddles from driftwood that washed ashore.
Most of the men would have been working in the village, while
the women would have been out collecting plants, wild fruits,
and small fish. Children and dogs ran everywhere.

villagers probably celebrated there, too, because we found discarded deer bones and broken pottery from the feasts. There was a big supply of red ochre (red pigment) in the mound where they'd been storing it. Red was a very important color.

Over in the other mound, we found the remains of the charnel house where they'd stored the bones. Lots of pots were there, too, special kinds of pottery they might have used for drinking sacred teas.

The bones of the woman were in the third mound. She had been shot in the left hip with an arrow; archaeologists found the point still embedded on the bone. She had probably died of an infection from the wound. "She was buried in a crypt in a grave with a little tomb in the floor of her house. The house was burned on top of this and covered with a big mound of dirt," Milanich says.

At some point, probably at the death of the woman, the village decided to close down the area. Milanich continues, "On the other two mounds, the bones were taken from one and put across clean sand. Then they were covered up with another mound to make a monument. The mound where they'd built the facility for cleaning the bones was also destroyed, then burned, then covered. It was extraordinary."

Most Florida groups, especially the southern ones, moved their villages every few years. Houses got old, the garbage piled too high, and everything started to smell bad, especially in summer. Dr. Milanich observes that "Often near a village, you'll find a dump, just like in medieval times in London. Not too far from the village, off to one side. The garbage just piled up." When things got bad enough, each family packed its belongings and headed to another village site, usually only a few miles away. The families stayed there for twenty or thirty years, until that village got old and began to smell bad. Then they would move again, sometimes back to the place where they had lived before, and start over. "It's clear that people reoccupied locations. They, like anyone else, wanted to live in a good place that had access to three things: fresh water, for drinking; the shore, where they collected fish and other seafood; and good hunting areas. They were very smart; they selected the best locations, where it was easiest to make a living," says Dr. Milanich.

FOOD

Peoples of North America—and especially Florida tribes—had vast resources for food and hundreds of years of knowledge in how to prepare it. In many ways, they ate better then than many Americans do today, for they had the entire uncontaminated North American continent to provide them with supplies. Food from the freshwater lakes and rivers and marine life from the sea sustained all the Florida American Indians. Freshwater rivers, lakes, and streams gave them catfish, trout, snails, and turtles. The saltwater marshes, the swamps, and the sea itself teemed with every imaginable kind of fish and shellfish: clams, mussels, oysters, lobsters, crabs, sharks, and countless kinds of fish.

The northern peoples supplemented their diet of seafood with crops. The Timucua of northern Florida planted fields and gardens of maize, beans, peas, pumpkins, citrons (yellow fruits that look like lemons), and gourds. Historical accounts describe how in the spring, usually in April, men and women cleared the land, sometimes cutting down trees and burning them to make new fields. This also flushed out small game and made it easy to hunt. They burnt plant matter, it hoed into the ground for fertilizer, then planted the seeds.

During the growing months, field-workers (usually women but sometimes men as well) weeded and maintained the fields with hoes—each one made of a wooden handle tipped with large fish bones. In some villages, there were small houses built on each corner of the field. All summer, lookouts lived there and watched for animals and birds that would try to destroy the crops.

The corn was harvested twice a year, once in the late spring and again in the fall. Some of the corn was picked, then stored in bins still on the cob. Most of the corn was shelled and made into cornmeal. Women had the hard job of grinding the corn into meal, which they did by using large wooden mortars and pestles two feet long. This cornmeal was the basic ingredient of most dishes cooked by the northern Florida peoples. They ate it in stews, baked it in cakes such as cornbread, and served it as a porridge mixed with water and animal fat.

Peoples in north and south Florida also foraged for wild edible plants, and the list of what they gathered for food is most impressive: acorns, hickory nuts, palm berries, walnuts, wild grapes, hazelnuts, wild cherries, plums, persimmons, blueberries, huckleberries, elderberries, peppervine, ground-cherries, pokeweed, broomweed, sunflowers, and all kinds of roots. Archaeologists find the pits and seeds of these fruits at village sites. The people also mixed hickory-nut meal with parched cornmeal and dried berries to make a kind of "trail mix" that hunters and field workers ate as they tracked game and tended the fields for days at a time.

The Everglades and wetlands of the south provided the Calusa with an abundance of food. They used large nets weighted down with bone and stone to catch shellfish, sharks, many kinds of fish, and reptiles, including alligators. Some Spanish documents describe how fish were also caught with elaborate weirs—mesh frames of split saplings tied with sinew, used for trapping river fish—traps, and spears. The weirs could be up to 250 yards long. They were placed in streams that emptied into marshes or coastal lagoons, which rose and fell with the tide. Fishermen opened the weirs during high tide, then closed them as the tide went down, trapping the fish inside.

Because of the hot, humid weather, fresh food tended to spoil fast. Fish especially didn't keep for long. The south Florida tribes spent a lot of time drying and smoking their catch by placing it on large wooden racks above smoldering fires. They also dried fish by laying them on tall, upright wooden racks built throughout the village.

DECEPTIVE DRAWINGS

One of the most precious resources for an archaeologist studying precontact American Indian societies is the written records of the early explorers. But these documents can be full of inaccuracies and errors—and they were, of course, written after contact. Only careful scrutiny can separate what is likely to be true from what is false. One such record is known as the DeBry (dee BREE) illustrations. Its saga began near present-day Jacksonville, Florida. During the early days of exploration, many European countries raced to claim a piece of this vast new world. England, France, and Spain all sent ships filled with colonists and explorers to settle and conquer. In the 1560s, a group of French explorers were living at Fort Caroline. With them was a cartographer and painter named Jacques LeMoyne. In October 1564, the fort was raided by Pedro Menéndez de Avilés, a Spaniard who drove out the French and claimed Fort Caroline for Spain. LeMoyne was one of the lucky few who escaped.

Back in France, LeMoyne painted from memory a series of watercolors of the Florida peoples. He died soon after, in 1588, leaving all his drawings to his wife. Desperate for money after her husband's death, she sold the watercolors to the DeBry family. They were publishing a series of books on the Americas and the LeMoyne artwork was just the thing they needed. The LeMoyne drawings appeared in one of the books, redone as engravings.

DeBry had decided to "improve" LeMoyne's work and redrew many of the watercolors. However, he had never even been to America. Based on what he had heard about the New World, he added South American headdresses and clubs to some of the drawings—objects that were from the Amazon, not Florida. In some drawings, French soldiers even have their helmets on backward! When

Game was part of the diet of every Florida tribe as well, but some people depended on it more than others. Deer was the most important meat source, but people also ate duck, goose, loon,

Florida people preparing a field. Although there are many inaccuracies in this drawing, scientists can glean much information from it about how Florida people tended their crops. *(New York Public Library)*

DeBry drew people drinking from shell cups, he showed them using the wrong kind of shells. Their bodies and faces have a romanticized European look, almost as if they were sculptures come to life.

But DeBry managed to keep some details accurate. For example, the woodcut above shows people preparing and planting a field. The people are unrealistic and the clothing is probably stylized, but a close look at their tools and actions reveals important clues. The women are using sticks to poke holes into the earth for the seeds. The men are using hoes that look to be made from wood or bone, much like real tools that archaeologists have found. Combined with written records and archaeological evidence, the DeBry woodcuts can provide archaeologists with new understanding of how tools were used and who may have used them.

pelican, turkey, raccoon, squirrel, rabbit, possum, bear, fox, panther, and bobcat. Archaeologists usually find the bones of these animals in a village garbage dump.

Most hunters used bows and arrows to kill their prey. The bows, sometimes as tall as a man, were made of wood and strung with animal gut. Arrows were wooden and tipped with sharp fish bone or shell points. Skilled craftsmen also made spears of wood with fish bone, shark teeth, and shell tips.

Hunting parties set out for weeks at a time, building temporary hunting camps in the forests and killing and cleaning enough game to feed the village for weeks. Groups would also go on fishing expeditions, especially at times of the year when certain fish were running or the weather was good. Sea turtles were hunted during their egg-laying season, and their eggs were collected and taken back to the village.

Southern tribes, especially the Calusa, relied on one another for help during bad hunting seasons or times of trouble. If a coastal village, for example, had a bad fishing year or was hit by a hurricane, the people of that village might send word to those who lived in villages in the interior, who would send dried foods and smoked meats. And if inhabitants of an interior village needed help, or if they just wanted seafood from the coast, their coastal neighbors quickly brought supplies in for them.

SOCIETY

European accounts of Florida societies usually single out specific "kings," or chiefs, who seemed to run things in a village or city. The Spanish thought of a king as an absolute ruler, with the ability to control his subjects. They therefore assumed that the American Indian chiefs they encountered had the same power. They also assumed that all chiefs were men. Both of these assumptions were wrong.

American Indian societies in general, and Florida groups in particular, had a variety of ways of governing their people. Larger, agricultural areas with many citizens had more complex systems than did the smaller villages in the southern wetlands.

In the northern areas, most people lived in small to middle-sized villages, and each village had its chief and village leaders. These people governed by council, meeting and discussing affairs of the village and agreeing on a course of action. Sometimes, larger villages might split and form separate towns. They would, however, remain closely tied together through kinship and a common history. The chiefs of the new villages joined with the others to form an informal political group. In this way, over generations, many small villages stayed connected through friendship, kinship, and mutual trust.

Although these chiefs were equal in status to one another, the reality was that one person, perhaps the chief of the largest village, or one who commanded the greatest respect, might have the most power and influence. As villages grew, especially in the northern areas, where some agricultural cities could have as many as 50,000 citizens, this chief became the principal leader in the region. In his book *The Timucua,* Dr. Milanich quotes Father Francisco Alonso de Jesús as he describes the Spanish view of Timucua chiefs in 1630.

In this scene, council members drink Black Drink before deliberations. This caffeine-laden beverage was made from a special holly berry and drunk before battle and during council sessions. It sometimes induced vomiting, which was thought to cleanse the body. *(New York Public Library)*

They have their natural lords among them . . . these gov-
ern their republics as head with the assistance of counsel-
lors, who are such by birth and inheritance. [The chief]
determines and reaches decisions on everything that is
appropriate for the village and the common good with
their accords and counsels.

Rituals and tradition dictated how a chief behaved toward the villagers and how they responded. Chiefs didn't stand up to greet any visitors (or anyone else, for that matter) they felt were below them in status. Instead, they offered gifts to their visitors as a greeting and a show of respect. Some chiefs were carried through-out the villages on litters made of wood and covered with palm fronds and boughs. Carrying the chief was a job for people with high status in the village, such as members of high-ranking fami-lies. Musicians proceeded the chief, playing flutes to let the people know the chief was coming.

In the northern areas of the Timucua, chiefs and their families usually lived atop large earthen mounds built especially for them. The chief had a special seat in the council house, where village business was conducted and decisions were made. Chiefs were also greeted in a special way.

Most leaders and their families were elaborately tattooed with symbols of their clan and of their status. Copper ornaments, imported from as far away as the Great Lakes, were prized. Chiefs and their kin were the only ones allowed to wear certain bird plumes, and bearskin hides were also reserved for the chief and his or her family.

A chief could be either a man or a woman, since the right to rule was passed from the mother's family. Most Florida societies were divided into clans that consisted of families who were related through the women. This way of recognizing relation-ships in societies, called matrilineal, was the norm throughout North America before European contact. In matrilineal societies, the right of inheritance, including the right to rule, was passed down from the mother rather than the father. Children were considered members of their mother's clan rather than their

"Saturiova, King of Florida" was a Timucua leader. In this sketch by Jacques LeMoyne, Saturiova is decorated with elaborate tattoos and wears a pelt. He is probably dressed for combat. The cup in his hand may contain Black Drink. *(Peabody Museum, Harvard University/photo by Hillel Burger)*

father's. A woman's brothers were in charge of raising her children, teaching them the skills needed to survive. Inherited titles were passed down through a person's uncles (on the mother's side) instead of the father.

Chiefs inherited their power from their mother's lineages, but chiefs weren't always men. In many Timucua tribes, women were chiefs. They had the same power and commanded the same respect as their male counterparts. During council meetings, Dr. Milanich explains in *The Timucua*, "when . . . a cacia [woman chief] is the one in charge and the lord of the land . . . she sits alone on her seat and the rest of the women sit separated from the men." Spanish and French explorers never really grasped the idea that women could rule in their own right. Many European documents say that a women chief was the widow of a male chief who had died. This was almost never the case.

EUROPEAN CONTACT

In 1513, a little more than 20 years after Columbus first sighted the New World, members of the Calusa tribe saw their first European. He was a Spanish explorer by the name of Juan Ponce de León.

He and his crew landed in a number of places, never staying long in one spot. Everywhere they went, they destroyed towns, burned crops, and either killed or enslaved the inhabitants. They stayed in Florida a little more than three weeks before heading back to Puerto Rico, where the Spanish had already settled. Ponce de León returned in 1521 to establish a colony in southwest Florida, meeting opposition. Deadly battles between the Spanish and the Calusa resulted in many deaths on both sides. During one battle, Ponce de León was wounded by an arrow. He ordered his crews to retreat to Cuba, where he died from his injuries.

Although Ponce de León's exploration had ended in his death, news of his initial successes in conquering the New World opened the floodgates of exploration by Europeans. Rumors of riches from members of León's expedition became too tempting to ignore. Missionaries, colonists, explorers, adventurers, thieves, and businessmen descended on Florida. Captured and sold into slavery, decimated by disease and warfare, and relocated far from their homes, the Florida peoples were no match for the sheer numbers of the Europeans, their guns, and most important, their diseases, such as smallpox. By 1710—less than 200 years after Ponce de León's 1513 expedition—most of the Native American people who had once roamed the forests, beaches, wetlands, and fields of Florida were gone.

NOTES

p. 3   "In Florida, there were extreme variations . . ." Dr. Jerald Milanich, curator in archaeology, Florida Museum of Natural History, Gainesville, interview by Allison Lassieur (May 1997).

p. 4   "Archaeologists trace Timucuan culture . . ." Dr. Dean Snow quoted in Alvin M. Josephy Jr., ed., *America in 1492* (New York: Vintage Books, 1991), p. 141.

p. 5   "Numerous references . . ." Milanich, *The Timucua* (Cambridge, Massachusetts: Blackwell Publishers, 1996), p. 56.

p. 6   "Agriculture comes into north Florida . . ." Milanich, interview (February 1997).

p. 6   "[They were] circular in shape . . ." Milanich, *The Timucua*, p. 24.

p. 9   "[winter] houses in the summer . . ." Milanich, interview (February 1997).

p. 9   "Shell deposits . . ." Milanich, *Archaeology of Pre-Columbian Florida* (Gainesville: University Press of Florida, 1994), p. 243.

pp.10–11 "This was a site . . ." Milanich, interview (February 1997).

p. 11   "Often near a village . . ." Milanich, interview (Febuary 1997).

pp. 11–12 "It's clear that people reoccupied . . ." Milanich, interview (Febuary 1997).

p. 18   "They have their natural lords among them . . ." Father Francisco Alonso de Jesús, quoted in Milanich, *The Timucua*, p. 158.

p. 20   "when . . . a cacia . . ." Milanich, *The Timucua*, p. 157.

IN THE WOODLAND REALM

PEOPLE OF THE EASTERN WOODLANDS

The American Indians of the Northeast were among the first people who met the Europeans who came to America to explore and colonize the "New World." They taught the first settlers how to grow crops, what plants to pick, and how to hunt in the dense forests. Without this help, it is likely that few Europeans would have survived America.

The first European that some Northeast peoples met was probably Italian explorer Giovanni da Verrazano, who sailed the East Coast in 1524. When he described the land he saw, he didn't know that he was recording a place that was home to hundreds of thousands of people. They spoke as many as 68 different languages. They lived in tiny hamlets of a few longhouses, small villages of a few hundred, and large cities of thousands. The area of the Northeast, broken by mountains, rivers, farmlands, and forests, provided the people with a bounty of resources. These natural boundaries throughout the area that separated the different groups also dictated how they lived, what they ate, and how they conducted their lives.

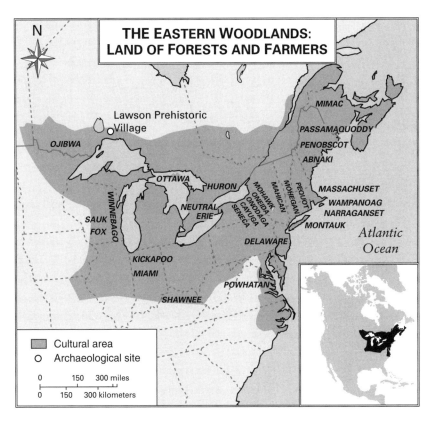

THE EASTERN WOODLANDS: LAND OF FORESTS AND FARMERS

N

Lawson Prehistoric Village

MIMAC
PASSAMAQUODDY
PENOBSCOT
ABNAKI
OJIBWA

OTTAWA
HURON
NEUTRAL
ERIE
MOHAWK
MAHICAN
ONEIDA
CAYUGA
ONONDAGA
SENECA
MOHEGAN
PEQUOT
MASSACHUSET
WAMPANOAG
NARRAGANSET
MONTAUK
DELAWARE

WINNEBAGO
SAUK
FOX

Atlantic Ocean

KICKAPOO
MIAMI
POWHATAN
SHAWNEE

Cultural area
O   Archaeological site

0   150   300 miles
0   150   300 kilometers

Unbroken forests that stretched from the Atlantic coast to the fringes of the Great Plains met early Europeans who landed in the Northeast. This area was home to the powerful Iroquois Confederacy, then a group composed of the Five Nations, who created a democracy that some believe was the inspiration for the United States' system of government.

LAND

The vast Eastern Woodlands extended for nearly 1 million square miles, from the shores of the Atlantic north through what is now Canada, west to the Great Lakes and beyond, and south to present-day North Carolina. Throughout this region are many kinds of landscapes: beaches, rocky coastlines, dense forests, mountain ranges, meadowlands, lakes, rivers, and swamplands. The eastern boundary of this region is the Atlantic coastal plain, where some of the most complex cultures lived and farmed. This area stretched from the cool Atlantic coastline to the mighty Mississippi River. The northern area ran across what is now Canada into present-day Minnesota and Wisconsin and included southern Ontario, upper New York state, and the St. Lawrence and Susquehanna valleys. Here, cooler temperatures made farming more difficult. But massive herds of deer, elk, moose, and other game were plentiful. Millions of passenger pigeons, now extinct, turned the sky black with flocks that took days to pass overhead. The rivers teemed with salmon, sturgeon, and trout. Bushes drooped under the weight of blackberries, huckleberries, and raspberries.

The central northeastern areas included the areas around the Great Lakes and dipped south into what are now Ohio, Kentucky, and West Virginia. Southward, mountain ranges such as the Cumberland and the Blue Ridge were filled with thousands of valleys, hollows, and hidden meadows where people hunted and grew corn, beans, and squash.

PEOPLE

The peoples of the Eastern Woodlands were vastly different from one another, yet they shared many traits. The tribes of the coastal areas were Algonquian speakers and included the ancestors of the Micmac, Delaware, Abnaki, Narraganset, Penobscot, and many others. The Iroquoian-speaking people of the Great Lakes regions—including the Mohawk, Oneida, Onondaga, Cayuga, Seneca, Huron, Neutral, and Erie—took advantage of both the water's resources and the rich soil of the boggy bottomlands. They were farmers as well as fishermen, raising corn, beans, and squash—the "Three Sisters" of American Indian agriculture.

The tribes in the central areas around the Great Lakes and present-day Ohio, Kentucky, and West Virginia spoke Siouan languages and included the ancestors of what are now the Shawnee, Kickapoo, Miami, Winnebago, and Mesquakie (formerly Fox). These tribes farmed a little but relied more on a combination of farming and hunting for their livelihoods.

The Micmac, like many of the northern tribes, relied on furs and skins for clothing. Early European accounts describe their wearing clothing cut from the belly skin of moose and made into jacketlike shirts that belted around the waist. The western Abnaki also wore clothes made of fur and skins.

The clothing styles of the Virginia Algonquians was based on rank. Some people went naked, while others wore either a belted leather breechcloth (men) or a deerskin apron (women). The upper class wore fringes on their deerskin clothing, and their upper garments were fringed, beaded, and decorated with porcupine quills and feathers. Everyone had a deerskin or rabbit-skin cloak that fastened over one shoulder and was worn fur side in for warmth. They also wore breechcloths and leggings made of leather. Some people also wore elaborate coats made of turkey feathers. The upper classes owned precious copper beads, which were probably imported from as far away as the Great Lakes. These beads decorated clothing, shoes, and other objects. Occasionally, an archaeologist finds stray beads at a dig site. Someone probably lost or dropped the beads, because they are sometimes found in unlikely places, such as in a garbage pit or an unused corner of a house site.

Hairstyles varied greatly from tribe to tribe. Accounts describe the Micmac as wearing their hair long. They rarely wore any kind of headgear. Many of the women of the Algonquian tribes shaved the front and sides of their head, leaving one section of hair that they wore in long braids. Men usually shaved the right side of their head, so that their bow-strings wouldn't get caught in their hair.

Men rarely grew beards, preferring instead to pluck out facial hair with two shells used as tweezers. Most tribes, especially those who spent most of their time outdoors in the fields, covered themselves with bear grease or oil made from acorns and walnuts. This was used both as a sunblock and an insect-repellent. Both men and women had tattoos.

Capitaine de la Nation des Illinois, Il est armé de sa pipe, et de son dard.

This drawing of an Illinois man was done about 1700 by Louis Nicolas, a Jesuit priest. The man has designs either tattooed or painted on his body, and he holds an elaborately decorated pipe and a spear. *(From the collection of Thomas Glicrease Museum, Tulsa, Oklahoma)*

Sauuage de La Nation des onneiothéaga. Il fume, du tabac a l'honneur du soleil quil adore comme son genie particulier f.14.

This drawing, by Louis Nicolas, shows an Oneida warrior smoking a pipe and carrying a tobacco pouch. Nicolas wrote that this man was honoring the sun. He wears a decorated loincloth and a headband. *(Newberry Library, Chicago)*

VILLAGES

Most Eastern Woodland tribes were farmers. They built their villages near good farming ground, which was usually fertile river-bottom land. Many villages were built on bluffs or hills overlooking the fields and a river or a stream. A number of village sites that archaeologists study today are found in these places. The northern tribes, who relied more on hunting, built their homes and villages near fresh water and within easy walking distance of the best hunting grounds.

North Carolina Algonquians built their villages either around a central plaza or scattered in their cornfields. Scientists find anywhere from 10 to 30 houses in a village, which was usually near a water source such as a river or a lake. When water was scarce, these Algonquians sometimes dug ponds for water. Many villages, especially those on boundaries between tribal lands where warfare was common, built strong palisades of sharpened posts around their villages. People threw their trash in huge garbage heaps, or middens, outside these walls. Inside were homes, storage facilities, religious structures, and other public buildings.

After 15 or 20 years in one place, even a small village would exhaust the resources of an area. The rich fields would be depleted of their nutrients, and crops would begin to fail. Game in the forests nearby would be gone. When the time came, the tribe then abandoned its village site and built a new one, usually only a day's walk away. When the villagers decided to move, the women set out to select the new place. Once they chose the land and the fields, the men went to the site and began building. Everyone lived in their old homes until building was complete. Then as each home was finished, the family packed its belongings, carried them to the new village, and moved in.

The design of the houses depended on who built them and where the people lived. The most common form of structure, used by most of the Iroquoian-speaking tribes, was the longhouse. Pages of documents written by Europeans—especially Jesuit priests who lived in the area—describe these houses in detail. Longhouses tended to be about 80 feet long, 20 feet wide, and 20 feet high, but the length depended on how many families lived there. At the London Museum of Archaeology in Ontario, Canada, Dr. Robert Pearce has studied how some northeastern tribes built their homes. The first thing he looks for at a dig site is post holes.

He explains, "There's visible evidence of where posts were in the ground. The circular stains left by the posts follow a pattern, and that's where the walls were. So we know where each wall post was and can tell exactly how long and wide a house was." Archaeologists also call these post molds.

But the evidence can give only part of the picture. Dr. Pearce relies on ethnographic evidence to complete the scene.

He continues, "From the archaeological evidence, you don't have any idea how high a house might have been. But we know from documents from Jesuit priests that Iroquoian houses were as tall as they were wide. So we can reasonably guess that these houses must have been 20 feet high."

Many European documents describe how a longhouse was built. The men of the clan built the houses. First, they cut down two large trees as support posts, one for each end of the long-house. Smaller wall posts formed the rectangular shape of the house. Tree saplings were lashed to these posts and bent from one long side of the rectangle to the other, making a barrel roof. When that was done, the men laid bark mats over the frame, covering the walls and roof. There weren't any windows in a longhouse, just a door at one end of the building and smoke holes in the roof.

Inside, an area like a hallway ran down the center. There were three to five separate cooking fires in this area, and each fire was shared by two families. On either side of this hallway were small apartment-like rooms, with one family in each apartment. So a typical longhouse might be home to as many as 10 families at once.

In each apartment, attached to the back wall, were sleeping plat-forms about three feet off the ground. "Inside these houses, we find evidence of small support posts, about three or four inches in diameter," says Dr. Pearce. They're usually about three feet away from the wall of the house. Some of the written evidence describes how these posts supported sleeping platforms."

Documents describe grass mats, furs, and blankets woven from animal hair that were on the beds, making things comfort-able for everyone. The space underneath the platforms was used to store food, extra weapons, clothing, and personal items.

In some North Carolina Algonquian houses, there were long shelves above the platforms with racks for gear and food. Between apartments, and sometimes in the corners of the longhouse, stood large basketry bins of bark or other materials and filled with corn and other dried foods. Sometimes archaeologists find the remains of these food-storage bins, so they are able to pinpoint exactly where people stored their food in the house. Firewood was stacked near the doorway in little vestibules, ready for use.

Tribes in the northern areas of Canada, Maine, and Vermont built round houses instead of rectangular ones. The Micmac had large, conical wigwams covered with animal skins, bark, and sometimes evergreen branches. The Abnaki, who lived in villages that dotted the coastal areas from North Carolina all the way to Nova Scotia, built two kinds of houses. Some were round with a circular floor. They built others in a shape like a pyramid with a square floor. They were permanent structures, covered with sheets of bark. These houses had two doors, one left open all the time for the smoke from the center hearth to escape.

Longhouses were more than just living spaces. They defined the Iroquoian families who lived in them. People sharing a long-house were most likely related to one another and part of the same clan. Grandparents, parents, aunts and uncles, and cousins lived alongside one another. They believed that their family was linked spiritually through sacred animals as well as by blood through the lineage of the women of the clan.

FOOD

A common view of Indians is that they were hunters or foragers, scouring the land for whatever food they could find. Centuries before Europeans looked upon the vast, fertile fields of the New World, the American Indian tribes who lived here had been working the land. For them, farming was a way of life.

The climate and resources of each region dictated what crops people grew. In the chilly north, where the growing season was short and cool, the Micmac and the Maliseet-Passamaquoddy of Maine and New Brunswick planted small gardens. Farther south, where the weather was milder, corn crops were huge and the growing season lasted throughout the summer. In the western fringes of the Eastern Woodlands, in present-day Wisconsin and Minnesota, people gathered wild rice to supplement their diet of game and plants.

The Iroquoian and Algonquian tribes began preparing the fields in the spring by slash-and-burn agriculture. After a good field was chosen, the men cleared it of all the leaves and branches. Then they burned the land and hoed all the ashes, partially burnt wood, and other charred forest debris into the ground, giving the soil natural fertilizer.

Around March or April, women began breaking up the fields with hoes made of clam shells or deer scapulae (shoulder blades). These shells or bones were lashed onto wooden handles and looked very much like hoes used today. Broken parts of hoes are

This Mohican pot is shaped like a squash. This type of ground-growing squash, which needs good soil and shady areas, thrives underneath the shade of corn and beans—the "Three Sisters" of American Indian agriculture. *(The Field Museum, Chicago, Neg #A 44300)*

sometimes found at dig sites. Many look remarkably like the way they are described in some accounts. In some Algonquian tribes, both men and women worked the fields. After the fields were broken up, women and children planted the corn. Usually a few kernels were planted into a small mound of earth, making the fields look full of small bumps by the time they were done. Along with the corn, they planted squash and beans.

Once the crops were planted, some members of the tribe took on the job of field watching. Their duty was to weed the fields and chase away animals and birds all summer. In some Algonquian tribes, the field watchers lived right in the middle of the fields on small open platforms.

In summer, women spent their days scouring the forests for raspberries, blueberries, strawberries, blackberries, and grapes; nuts such as hickory nuts, chestnuts, acorns, and walnuts; edible plants for food and for medicine; honey; and other foods. The women dried the berries and stored them in bark containers or made them into dried, pounded cakes shaped like disks that could be eaten year-round.

During all times of the year, but especially in the cooler months, women made thick stews of meat and vegetables. First, they put a few stones into the fire to heat them. Then they filled a large bark bucket with water. Using tongs, they carefully pulled the red-hot stones from the fire and dropped them into the water, making it boil. To this they added the meat, vegetables, and seasonings. When one rock cooled, it was taken out and another added until the stew was done.

Dr. Pearce says, "We find thousands of broken firestones all over sites. When hot rocks are put into water, sometimes they shatter like an ice cube. That tells us that this method of cooking was used a lot."

All American Indian tribes relied on wild game. Moose and caribou were plentiful in the northern areas. Micmac hunters broke up into small groups to hunt these enormous animals. They also built snares to trap partridge and water birds, seal, beaver, rabbit, otter, and porcupine.

To hunt moose, Micmac hunters made callers out of birch bark. On dark nights during the mating season, they made the call of the female moose, then carefully poured water on the ground from a birch bark dish. The male moose heard the noises of the call and the water, thought it was a female moose urinating, and would come to investigate.

The Iroquoians, Algonquians, and other more southern tribes relied on deer for a great deal of their meat. European accounts describe how hunting parties built large three-sided corral-like compounds out of branches and saplings. On either side, they added a long wooden fence angled out from the opening of the corral. The hunters then chased deer, herding them into this corral, where they could be killed more easily.

Most hunters used bows and arrows, snares, nets, and spears to hunt game. Abnaki hunters usually carried a bow and arrow, a long lance, and a knife made of sharpened stone or bone. Hanging from a leather belt slung over the shoulder was a game bag, usually made of leather, and a smaller bag made of woodchuck skin containing a fire-making kit. They also carried dried corn cakes and dried berries in their leather pouch as a sort of trail mix to eat during the hunt.

Fishing was the domain of the men, and they built elaborate weirs. Lake fishermen made large nets and cast them into the water from large dugout canoes. Fishermen used fishing poles and harpoons as well.

"We've found objects that look like harpoons," says Dr. Pearce. "Tiny pieces of bone, sharpened at both ends, are stuck in a shaft point up. When you stick them in a large fish and pull up, the fish can't get off."

Once the hunters had returned to the village with game and fish, the women took over. Meat and fish were either smoked or eaten fresh by most tribes. The Virginia Algonquians roasted seafood and shellfish or boiled it in a broth. The Micmac roasted meat, fish, and eels or boiled them in large wooden troughs made from tree trunks. Sometimes they cooked meat by hanging it by a twisted cord over a fire. The cord rotated as it slowly untwisted.

Animal hides were used for clothes, bedding, pouches, and other leather items. Antlers made good tools, beads, and other ornaments. Bones were scraped, cleaned, and used for hoes, tools, and jewelry. Archaeologists often find broken tools and small beads made of antler and bone at a village site. Animal stomachs and bladders were removed, cleaned, and used as waterproof containers. Guts were cleaned and cut into strips, then used as lashings. Feathers, porcupine quills, and animal claws and teeth were all removed, cleaned, and used to decorate clothing and objects. Nothing was wasted.

SOCIETY

The longhouse symbolized the society of the Iroquoian-speaking people of the Northeast, both to themselves and to the Europeans who first met them. Each longhouse held a clan whose members were tied to one another by blood relations and long traditions. Europeans were fascinated by a culture so alien to theirs, and they left us many records of how they perceived American Indian life.

Clans in all northeastern tribes were matrilineal; kinship was recognized through the women of the family. Women owned the property, the house, the land, and all the food grown on it. Children were recognized as members of their mother's clan. They weren't considered to be related to anyone in their father's clan.

Micmac women usually gave birth outside, away from the wigwam. The mother kneeled on the ground, helped by women of her mother's family. The newborn was washed in a cold stream, then placed in an ornamental cradleboard. Babies born into one of the Virginia Algonquian tribes received one name at birth. During a person's lifetime he or she might be given other names, symbolizing a skill or a special attribute.

Marriages were arranged but not forced. In the Maliseet-Passamaquoddy tribes, a man interested in marriage first talked it over with his relatives. When they found a suitable woman, he went to her home, where she was waiting. If he liked what he saw, he put a chip or stick in her lap. If she liked him, she returned the

An explorer named Alexander de Batz painted this watercolor of Illinois Indians in 1735. The chief wears a green necklace and a red breechcloth. The squatting man is a dancer, and he holds rattles made of squash. The young boy on the right is an African American, probably a slave who escaped and was adopted by the tribe. *(Peabody Museum, Harvard University/photo by Hillel Burger)*

chip and wedding plans would begin. If he wasn't acceptable, the woman made a face and tossed the chip away.

When a man from a Northeast tribe decided to marry, he usually had to perform bride service in the home of his future father-in-law. For one or two years, he worked for the woman's family, hunting under her father's direction and proving that he could provide for a family. In some groups, the groom had to make gifts for the father, such as arrows, bows, or a canoe. After two people married, they went to live in the longhouse of the wife's family.

EUROPEAN CONTACT

Centuries before Italian explorer Giovanni da Verrazano became the first European to describe the East Coast, in 1524, other Europeans had tried to colonize the New World. In about 985,

THE GREAT PEACE MAKER AND THE FIVE NATIONS

Sometime between 1450 and 1550, five tribes of the Iroquois people—the Seneca, Cayuga, Onondaga, Oneida, and Mohawk—came together and formed a powerful political body they called the Five Nations. Until well into the 18th century, the Five Nations dominated what is now New York State, and the success of their democratic system of government influenced the likes of Thomas Jefferson and Benjamin Franklin.

There are many theories as to why the Five Nations joined in the first place. Some say they were simply tired of fighting one another. Others claim that the tribes didn't create their democracy alone—they must have begun their confederacy with help from the Europeans. The Iroquois legend of the Great Tree of Peace explains the origin of the Five Nations and the reasons behind its beginnings.

Before the great Confederacy, all the Iroquois nations fought one another. The people were weak and their enemies killed them. Then the Peace Maker came. His canoe was made of sparkling white stone that did not sink. The first people he met were hunters, and he told them to tell their chiefs that they should no longer fight. Then he went to a woman's home, and she fed him. He told her of peace and power and its three parts: justice, health, and law. He explained that there would be a long house, a council of nations, and peace and unity among them. The Peace Maker made her the mother of nations.

Then he came to the house of the Man Who Eats Humans. This man had put a kettle on the fire with meat of a human inside it. The Peace Maker climbed on the roof and looked down through the smoke hole. The Man Who Eats Humans looked into the kettle and saw the Peace Maker's face reflected in the water. But it was his own face, only wise and noble.

"That is not the face of someone who eats humans," he said. "I won't do that anymore." The Peace Maker came inside and

Norse explorers led by Leif Eriksson landed in Newfoundland in northeastern Canada. If the Viking sagas (stories) are to be believed, the Norsemen lived in North America for a few years before being driven out by local tribes.

told the man his message of peace and power. The Peace Maker made this man his messenger and told him to convince the chiefs of the Great Peace.

The most difficult part of his task was to convince a cruel magician, the Onondaga's chief, Atotarho. His body was twisted seven times and he had a mass of writhing snakes instead of hair. Because of this, the Peace Maker gave his messenger the name Hiawatha, which means He Who Combs. The Peace Maker knew that Hiawatha would convert the evil chief and comb the snakes from his hair.

The Peace Maker went out and converted the Mohawks. Hiawatha began his battle with Atotarho, but the evil chief killed Hiawatha's wife and daughter. Hiawatha, overcome by grief, retreated to the lake shore. The Peace Maker consoled him, and Hiawatha was freed from his grief.

The Peace Maker and Hiawatha then visited the Oneidas, the Cayugas, and the Senecas, and told them of the Great Law of Peace. All the Onondaga chiefs except Atotarho listened, too. The Peace Maker talked to Atotarho and told him he would be the chief of all the Council and the Keeper of the Council fire. Atotarho agreed to be chief and Hiawatha combed the snakes from his hair. The seven twists came out of his body.

The Peace Maker planted a pine tree and called it the Tree of Peace. Soon four roots spread out, in the four directions. When the roots were grown, the Peace Maker pulled the tree out of the ground, threw all war weapons in the hole, and planted the tree again. He put an eagle high in the top branches, and the eagle's job was to sound the alarm if evil approached.

Roots have spread out from the Tree of the Great Peace. One to the north, one to the east, one to the south, and one to the west. These are the Great White Roots, and their nature is Peace and Strength. If any man or any nation obeys the laws of the Great Peace . . . they shall be welcomed to take shelter beneath the tree.

But it was the Europeans in the 16th century, led by Verrazano, who had the greatest impact on the people of the Eastern Woodlands. The Europeans came for many different reasons. The Spanish wanted to conquer lands for gold and riches. The French

A VISION OF CONTACT

The Sauk leader Black Hawk was born in 1767 and became famous in 1832 for his fight to regain his Illinois homeland, which had been settled by whites. In 1833, a book, *Black Hawk: An Autobiography*, was published. In that book, Black Hawk describes his great-grandfather's dream about the coming of Europeans.

> My great grandfather, Nanàmakee, or Thunder, was born in the vicinity of Montreal, where the Great Spirit . . . inspired him with the belief that, at the end of four years, he should see a white man. . . . The Great Spirit came to him when he slept and directed him to take his two brothers and travel in a direction to the left of sun-rising. After pursuing this course for five days, he sent out his two brothers to listen if they could hear a noise. . . . Early the next morning they returned and reported that they had heard sounds which appeared near at hand. . . . They all started for the place; when reaching it Nanàmakee went alone to the place and found that the white man had arrived and pitched his tent. He [the white man] took him by the hand and welcomed him into his tent. He told him he [the white man] was the son of the King of France and that the Great Spirit had directed him to come here where he should meet a nation of people who had never yet seen a white man—that they should be his children, and he should be their father.

established trading posts and made fortunes trading fish and fur. English settlers wanted religious freedom and lands of their own to farm.

In the Northeast, at first, everyone lived in relative peace. Local tribes taught the settlers—many of whom had never hunted or farmed before in their lives—how to hunt and grow crops. In return, they were given metal tools, weapons, and other items that helped them in their daily lives.

Soon after the Europeans arrived, however, Native peoples began dying off in terrifying numbers. They didn't have any resistance to European diseases such as smallpox, measles, tuberculosis, chicken pox, and influenza and were ravaged by sickness. As tall-masted ships deposited wave after wave of Europeans on the New World's shore, the Northeast peoples were pushed farther and farther inland. Some tribes died out entirely. Others were so decimated that the people who were left joined other tribes. Still others, pushed out of their lands into the Plains areas, eventually became some of the nomadic tribes of the 19th century.

NOTES

p. 29   "There's visible evidence of where posts were . . ." Dr. Robert Pearce, curator, London Museum of Archaeology, Ontario, Canada, interview by Allison Lassieur (April 1997).

p. 29   "From the archaeological evidence . . ." Pearce, interview.

p. 29   "Inside these houses, we find evidence . . ." Pearce, interview.

p. 32   "We find thousands of broken firestones . . ." Pearce, interview.

p. 33   "We've found objects that look like harpoons . . ." Pearce, interview.

pp. 36–37 "Before the great Confederacy . . ." Quoted in D. M. Dooling and Paul Jordan-Smith, *I Became Part of It: Sacred Dimensions in Native American Life* (New York: Parabola Books, 1989), p. 32.

p. 38   "My great grandfather . . ." Black Hawk, quoted in Peter Nabokov, *Native American Testimony* (New York: Viking Penguin, 1978), p. 12.

MYSTERIES OF THE MOUNDS

PEOPLE OF THE SOUTHEAST

[The chief] already had much information from other Castellans [Spanish], and he knew very well about their lives and customs, which consist in occupying themselves like vagabonds in going from one land to another, living from robbing, pillaging, and murdering those who had not offended them in any way. He by no means desired friendship or peace with such people, but rather mortal and perpetual warfare. . . . He promised to wage war against them during all the time that they might see fit to remain in his province . . . by waylaying in ambushes, taking them off guard. He and all his people would die a thousand deaths to maintain their liberty.

—speech translated from an Ocale chief to
Hernando De Soto, 1539

It's clear from the Ocale chief's words that the people of the Southeast knew perfectly well what the Europeans were up to. The Spanish expedition led by Hernando De Soto in 1539 cut a swath of death and destruction across the region, and rumors of violent killings and rampant sickness at the hands of the Europeans traveled fast. Documents from De Soto's expedition record

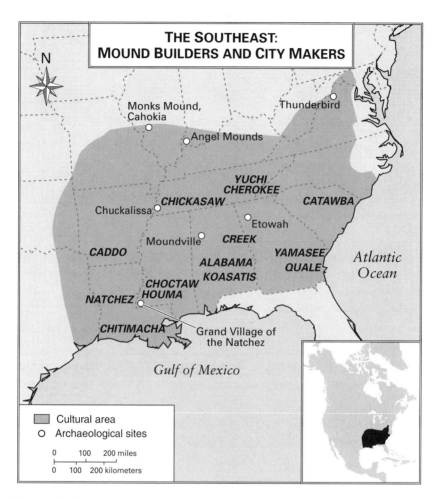

THE SOUTHEAST: MOUND BUILDERS AND CITY MAKERS

N

Monks Mound, Cahokia

Thunderbird

Angel Mounds

YUCHI
CHEROKEE
CHICKASAW
Chuckalissa

CATAWBA

Etowah

Moundville   CREEK

CADDO

ALABAMA
KOASATIS

YAMASEE
QUALE

Atlantic
Ocean

CHOCTAW HOUMA

NATCHEZ

CHITIMACHA

Grand Village of
the Natchez

Gulf of Mexico

Cultural area
O   Archaeological sites

0   100   200 miles
0   100   200 kilometers

The people of the Southeast built large cities of huge earthen mounds centuries before Europeans pushed through the forests to explore the area. Many of these mound cities, such as Etowah, Chuckalissa, and Moundville, still exist.

that the group encountered many abandoned villages and burnt fields—a testament to the fact that the people of the Southeast preferred destroying their homes and crops to being killed or enslaved by the Europeans.

Accounts from the expedition describe in detail what members saw as they tramped through the region. The thing that seemed to amaze the Europeans the most was the huge earthen mounds they sometimes passed. Some mounds, located inside villages, rose dozens of feet in the air and had impressive buildings constructed on their flat tops. Other mounds, standing alone, appeared to be long abandoned.

Oddly, although there are hundreds of documents describing these mounds, they were all but forgotten by the time European colonists began invading American Indian lands in the late 1700s.

The American Indians of the 18th century who met these colonists and explorers had no memory of the mounds, either. When the first Europeans questioned the local tribes about them, they were told that the earthen mounds that dotted the Southeast were the work of an ancient, giant race that had lived hundreds of years before them. Consequently, Europeans invented elaborate stories about the origins of the mounds—even suggesting that these mound complexes were so advanced that no American Indian tribe could have built them.

Many of these mounds still exist. Some of these flat-topped mounds are enormous, covering acres of land and rising as much as six stories above the ground. The largest mound in North America, Monks Mound, lies near the Mississippi River in present-day East St. Louis. Part of the mysterious Cahokia complex, Monks Mound is bigger at its base than is the Great Pyramid in Egypt. Other large mounds can be seen at Moundville in Alabama and Etowah in northwestern Georgia. Others are much smaller, some no more than bumps in a field or a forest. In many places, the mounds are situated in sophisticated layouts, a clear indication that they were placed deliberately and built with care.

A hundred years of archaeological exploration have helped to rediscover the origins of these mounds of earth. They were constructed by American Indian tribes known as the Mississippian cultures. The Mississippian groups dominated the region, and their network of cities and towns stretched from the shores of the Great Lakes in Illinois to the deltas of the Alabama and the Mississippi. Some of these tribes, including the Cherokee, Creek, Chickasaw, Caddo, and Choctaw, survive to this day.

Mound cities were religious and ceremonial centers and homes to thousands of people. The oldest cities, including Cahokia in Illinois, reached their peak in the 1300s. Then, inexplicably, most of the cities were slowly abandoned, until nothing remained but ruined buildings and the mounds they stood upon. Other cities, like the Grand Village of the Natchez in Mississippi, thrived long enough to be visited and documented by European explorers in the 1500s. Silent and green today, they are a mute testimony to a way of life that grew, flourished, and in some cases, died, before Europeans ever encountered them.

LAND

Mound cities can be found in Georgia, South Carolina, western North Carolina, Alabama, Mississippi, Louisiana, southern and eastern Arkansas, Tennessee, and parts of Missouri, Illinois, and Kentucky that border the Mississippi River. Many kinds of landscapes can be found in the Moundbuilders' homelands: mountains, prairies, forests, lakes, swamps, and coastlines. The one thing that links all these places, however, is the abundance of rich soil for farming. The river valleys surrounding the Mississippi are some of the most fertile lands in North America and have been so for centuries. Archaeologists and historians can look at the landscape today and imagine how it probably looked when precontact people lived there. Then, as now, the valleys renewed themselves every spring, when the high rivers receded and left fresh silt behind. This soft, rich soil was perfect for farming because it could be easily hoed and dug with sticks and wood-and-bone tools. Game such as deer, squirrel, raccoon, and turkey filled the forests near the rivers. During the year, the Mississippi River and its tributaries rose and sank with the seasons and the weather and created freshwater marshes and swamplands. These attracted large numbers of water birds and small water animals. The receding river waters also created natural ponds, where fish became trapped and could be easily caught.

In the areas between rivers and in places where the Mississippi curves inward upon itself, the constant rise and fall of the waters created lush meadow lands where nuts, fruit trees, and herbs thrived. These patches of open spaces surrounded by forests lined the Mississippi River for hundreds of miles, creating the perfect habitat for deer and a great abundance of foods that could be gathered and stored with relative ease. Although today most of the land on the Mississippi is full of factories, buildings, and other trappings of the 20th century, it once had this unique combination of farmlands and rich areas for hunting. That made this area the perfect setting for settlements that eventually became the huge mound cities of the Southeast.

PEOPLE

No one really knows how many people lived in the Mound-building cities of the Southeast before European contact. There could have been as many as 1.7 million inhabitants when the first explorers set foot there. The Timucua and the Apalachee lived in southern Georgia, the Guale made their homes along the Georgia coast, the Yamasee lived in South Carolina and parts of Georgia, and the Natchez, Houma and Chitimacha inhabited the area of the lower Mississippi River. These tribes were some of the first to be encountered by Europeans, beginning with De Soto's expedition in 1539. Their names are unfamiliar today because most of them were wiped out soon after the first wave of European explorers passed through.

Other tribes in the Southeast included the ancestors of the Cherokee of the southern Appalachians, the Catawba of South Carolina, the Chickasaw of northern Mississippi and southwestern Tennessee, the Caddo of Louisiana and Arkansas, and the Choctaw of southern Mississippi. Still other tribes, including the Creek, Alabama, Koasati, and Yuchi, lived along the rivers that snaked through the Southeast.

It is still something of a mystery who lived in southern Illinois, where some of the largest mound cities were abandoned in the 1300s. According to Dr. Brian Butler, a scientist at Southern Illinois University, "Because of dislocations and the depopulations that got serious in the late 16th and early 17th centuries, we have a hard time connecting known tribes with the late prehistoric archaeological record. By the time Europeans were in these areas and were describing what they saw, hardly anyone was living there."

Where did all the people go? That is one of the biggest dilemmas of modern archaeology. Dr. Mark Mehrer, an archaeologist at Northern Illinois University, explains, "We really don't have a clue about what happened at the end. It could have been a peasant revolt, or maybe the corn crop failed for several years in a row. But we don't see any evidence of a big conflict."

Not everyone disappeared, however. Scattered houses and

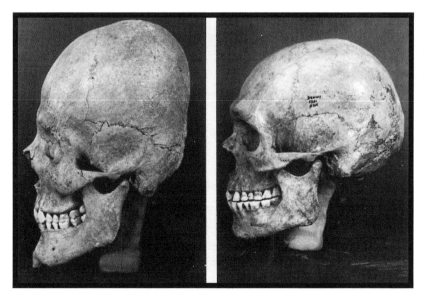

A sign of beauty and importance to many Moundbuilding people was a flat head. When a baby was born, he or she was bound to a cradleboard with a wooden brace. On the left is the flattened skull of a precontact American Indian, found near Nashville. On the right is a Native American skull from a late-18th-century site in South Dakota. *(Courtesy of William M. Bass, Department of Anthropology, University of Tennessee, Knoxville)*

small hamlets spread throughout the area attest to the fact that people lived on the land long after the huge cities faded away. Dr. Mehrer continues, "We still find domestic houses in the region. They are small sites, with one or two buildings each. By that time [the time the Europeans arrived], the things that remain are the scattered farmsteads out in the countryside."

This wasn't the case farther south, in the land of the Creek, Cherokee, and other southeastern tribes. While their villages weren't nearly as large or complex, they continued to build mounds and maintain a society that had its roots in the great cities of the northern areas. One city, the Grand Village of the Natchez in Mississippi, was the last surviving remnant of the grand mound cities that had thrived in the north in the 1300s. It existed until about 1730, when the French overwhelmed it. The Grand Village was described in detail by French explorers who visited it in the early 1700s.

Most of the people living in the mound cities were strong individuals. Europeans describe the men as tall, between 5 feet 10 inches and 6 feet. The women were usually shorter, and Creek women were seldom taller than 5 feet. Most men wore loincloths of leather in the summer, with small pouches hanging from belts around their waist. Women wove skirts out of grasses and Spanish moss for warm-weather wear.

In winter, the traditional article of clothing was a "matchcoat," an English pronunciation of an Algonquian word. This garment wasn't really a coat. Matchcoats, which were made of animal skins such as bison, beaver, and muskrat, were draped over the shoulders like capes and worn in very cold weather. For not-so-cold days, people wore matchcoats made of deerskin and painted with designs in red, yellow, and black.

Most people had tattoos, and many of the designs had religious or political significance. Scrolls, flowers, animals such as serpents, stars, crescents, and sometimes the sun (which was usually tattooed on the chest) were common. Creek chiefs divided their bodies into zones, where specific tattoos were placed. Dark blue or black tattoo ink was made from the soot of burning pitch pine, and red came from the mineral cinnabar. Some people made tattoos by pricking the skin with garfish teeth dipped in ink. Others preferred to use a comblike contraption made of five or six needles lined onto a small piece of wood.

VILLAGES

The villages and towns in which the precontact Moundbuilders lived were vastly different from one another. Each village had its own personality, look, and function, just as every town and city in North America today has its own identity.

The larger cities, such as Moundville, Etowah, and Angel, contained as many as 20 mounds, usually four-sided, of various sizes and heights depending on what they were used for. The chiefs, religious figures, and their families lived in residential complexes on top of the mounds. Some mounds also held temples and other ceremonial buildings where the elite of the city conducted business and performed rituals.

The mounds were made to impress all who saw them. Not only did they elevate the elite above the city physically, but the mounds were solid evidence of the political power of the chiefdoms. In *The Moundbuilders of Ancient America,* Robert Silverberg quotes the following description: "They build such sites with the strength of their arms, piling up very large quantities of earth and stamping on it with great force until they have formed a mound. . . . Then on the top of these places they construct flat surfaces which are capable of holding the ten, twelve, fifteen, or twenty dwellings of the lord and his family and the people of his service. At the foot of this hill . . . they construct a plaza, around which first the noblest and most important personages and then the common people build their homes."

At the base of the mounds was a plaza, the heart of the city. Today, visitors to some of the remaining mound cities, such as Moundville, can see where the plaza once was. Here people gathered to play games, to conduct citywide ceremonies, to trade,

DISK JOCKEYS

They're about the size of a hockey puck. They are carved from fine stone and polished to a high shine. They are chunkey disks, and they are small clues into the lives of the precontact peoples that used them in their most popular game.

Chunkey disk: This polished stone, about the size of a hockey puck, was used in a popular game called chunkey. *(Courtesy of the Frank H. McClung Museum, University of Tennessee, Knoxville)*

and to visit with one another. In some cities, the mounds and the plaza were surrounded by a palisaded wall of timber that might have stood up to 20 feet high. Scattered throughout the city were smaller mounds, where nobles, religious figures, and other important people lived. The rest of the town was made up of more public buildings, food-storage areas, and the homes of ordinary people. Sometimes archaeologists find a large number of specific objects, such as flint chips or broken pieces of pottery, in certain parts of town. This suggests that some cities might have been divided into districts, where residents held certain jobs such as pottery maker, basket maker, or toolmaker.

Surrounding the entire city was another large palisade, usually made of large posts set upright into the ground. Some documents

Chunkey was played only by the chief and other members of the village elite, often with crowds of spectators cheering on their favorite player. The game was played by two men, each with a pole. One player rolled the chunkey stone out onto the field. Just before the stone stopped, the men threw their poles at it, hoping to be the one whose pole landed nearest the stone when it fell.

The players were serious about their game. The Cherokee kept score by noting how close the chunkey stone landed to marks on the players' poles. In the Chickasaw version of the game, the pole nearest the stone got one point, but if the pole touched the stone, it meant two points. The object of the game for the Choctaw was to score 12 points.

Chunkey players had loyal followings and avid fans, just as sports figures do today. People gambled fiercely on chunkey, sometimes waging all their possessions on a single game. Some losers became so upset that they committed suicide.

Chunkey stones were owned by the entire town and carefully preserved. Archaeologists have found chunkey stones in the graves of chiefs and other elite members of the town. They've also discovered shell gorgets (ceremonial neck ornaments) carved with the images of chunkey players. These clues hint that chunkey was more than just a simple pastime. The game might have been part of an elaborate ceremony that archaeologists today can only guess at.

describe how smaller poles were attached to these horizontally. The whole thing was coated with a heavy layer of mud plaster, making an impressive fence around the town. Towers built along the wall could hold up to eight archers each, who manned the towers and defended the city during battle. Sometimes the city was encircled with a large ditch for defense.

Out in the countryside were scattered farms and villages, some quite large. In the northern areas, these villages had ceremonial mounds. People built their houses in rows with streets between them. Archaeologists can tell where the houses were by where they find post holes in the ground. In the eastern areas of Georgia and South Carolina, the villages were smaller, but they still built mounds for their important leaders.

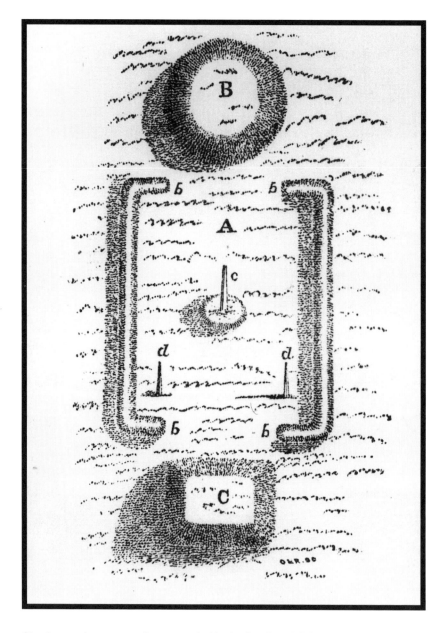

Chunkey yards were usually surrounded by banks of earth (b). A town house probably stood on the mound labeled (B). In the center of the court stood a tall pole (c), sometimes 30 to 40 feet high. In two corners of the yard stood slave posts (d) decorated with scalps and skulls and used to tie prisoners. *(Hargrett Library, University of Georgia Libraries)*

The Creek, Cherokee, Chickasaw, and other southern groups maintained substantial villages of their own. In these towns, council houses served as religious and ceremonial centers. One council house, excavated in Ocmulgee, Georgia, was one of the grandest that archaeologists had ever seen. In *America in 1492*, Peter Nabokov describes it: "It had a diameter of more than forty feet. Opposite a door was an earthen platform shaped like a giant bird of prey with shaped-clay seats for three people, while around the circumference were positions for another 47 individuals, probably the local chiefdom's senior statesmen."

Most people who lived in outlying areas and in smaller villages had two houses—a summer house and a winter dwelling, built near each other. The Creek, Chickasaw, and Cherokee dug a large circular hole about two or three feet deep, then built a framework of walls around it. The roof was made of notched poles attached to center posts and radiating out like the ribs of an umbrella. The roof and walls were covered with a plaster of mud clay mixed with grass or Spanish moss. The Chickasaw sometimes decorated their roofs by standing a pole with a carved animal, such as an eagle, on top. Dr. Mark Mehrer says, "We know that people made clay walls because sometimes when the houses burn down the clay fires out. We dig up chunks of burnt clay near wall trenches that tell us this."

European explorers were often surprised at how comfortable these houses were. They recorded numerous descriptions that help archaeologists reconstruct how these houses might have looked inside. Along the sides were sleeping platforms about two or three feet off the ground and piled with grass mats and furs. Small post holes that archaeologists find verify the descriptions left by Europeans. Sometimes the couches were angled slightly toward the wall, to keep a sleeping person from falling out of bed during the night. People stored food and personal belongings in baskets underneath these couches. In the center of the house was a large fire of very dry wood, which served as a cooking fire and as a way to heat the house.

The summer home was built for comfort in the hot, muggy southern summers. The Chickasaw built a framework of rot-resistant cypress or pine poles set in the earth. Fragments of the wood are sometimes still found. The roof was a lightweight framework of saplings, and roof shingles were lashed to the framework or weighted down with poles. Sometimes a space between the walls and roof was kept open to let in air. Inside, the walls were whitewashed with a mixture of crushed oyster shells and water, making them bright white and giving the inside a feeling of airiness.

FOOD

In the large cities, such as Moundville and Etowah, it was the chief's responsibility to store plenty of food reserves for hard times. He or she did this by requiring all citizens to pay taxes in the form of food at certain times of year. This food was stored in the cities' granaries and storehouses and shared by all during the winter, when food was scarce. Also, many city dwellers had small gardens for their families. They stored some of this food in small storage pits inside their homes.

European explorers described vast corn, or maize, fields, tended by farmers who lived near the fields year-round. The women were primarily responsible for the crops, although everyone in the village pitched in to help with spring planting. The best agricultural lands were in river valleys, which is why many of the largest cities that archaeologists study today are found near rivers.

Most agricultural lands were burned during the winter, fertilizing the soil and removing any brush and grasses that may have grown. In late spring, the workers broke up the fields with short-handled hoes made of wood and bone, usually the shoulder blade of a large animal, such as an elk or a bison. Many of these hoes were imported from farther north and were considered very valuable by the people who owned them. Today archaeologists find dozens of these tools at dig sites throughout the Southeast.

When the fields were ready, planting began. Workers used digging sticks to make holes in the soil, then dropped in seeds for corn, kidney beans, lima beans, squash, gourds, and pumpkins.

People also grew root vegetables, such as potatoes and yams. During the summer, workers lived in small huts near the fields, weeding the fields and guarding the tender plants from animals.

Women and children picked berries and gathered nuts during the summer and fall. Blackberries, palmetto gooseberries, grapes, mulberries, and wild cherries were gathered by the bushel and either eaten immediately or dried for later use. Nuts such as hickory nuts, walnuts, pecans, butternuts, and pawpaws were collected and stored.

All year long, hunters ventured into the forests to kill game. They went on hunting expeditions in groups, sometimes building small camps deep in the forest and living there for weeks. The most important game animal was deer, which provided not only meat, but hides, horns, and glue (from the horns and hooves). They also hunted wild turkeys, opossums, moles, black bears, raccoons, minks, skunks, badgers, red foxes, gray foxes, coyotes, timber wolves, cougars, swamp rabbits, woodchucks, squirrels, gophers, beavers, rats, muskrats, porcupines, otters, and snakes. People living near coastal areas also enjoyed alligator, crawfish, clams, mussels, fish, and turtle. Archaeologists find the bones of these animals near cooking pits in hundreds of homes they excavate, evidence of what the people who lived there ate and how much.

The primary hunting weapon was the bow and arrow. Bow makers fashioned bows from black locust or ash and strung them with sinew or buckskin. Arrows were made of cane or red dogwood tipped with flint points. The Natchez hunted bison and deer with arrows tipped with sharp bone points attached with sinew and glue. Wrist guards of leather or bark protected the hunter's arm from the sting of the bowstring. Accounts from de Soto's expedition include descriptions of the skill of the bowmen. Europeans were amazed at how accurate—and deadly—a bowman could be.

Although much of the food was grown and hunted for the entire village, each family was responsible for preparing its own meals. Most cooking was done in clay pots over a fire, and sometimes meat was roasted on a spit.

People roasted roots such as potatoes and sweet potatoes. They made thick stews filled with chunks of meat, vegetables, and wild herbs. Women made small cakes from dried fruits, such as raisins, persimmons, and figs, mashed with nuts and corn and soaked in bear fat. When they were thirsty, most people drank plain water, which came cold and pure from small springs and creeks. Sometimes they flavored the water with sweet herbs or made a tea from sassafras leaves.

In the 18th century, James Adair lived among the southeastern Indians and wrote about the foods that must have been eaten before Hernando de Soto's expedition showed up. One dish, a bread made by mixing cornmeal, beans, and sweet potatoes, was "baked either in thin cakes moistened with bear's oil, or as large loaves . . . the results were excellent," Adair reported.

SOCIETY

The Moundbuilders were a matrilineal culture—similar in that way to almost every society in North America prior to European contact. Families traced their ancestors through women, and the only relatives a person acknowledged were on the mother's side of the family. Houses, land, and property were controlled by the women of the clan. Men lived with their wife's family. A woman's brothers had great respect within the family and were responsible for bringing up their sister's children.

Most of what archaeologists and historians know about the customs of these people comes from the documents written by European explorers and priests who came to the area. Some of these customs were kept alive through oral tradition. Young women could get married at just about any age, but they usually waited until after they had had their first menstrual period. Young men were usually older before they proposed. If a man was interested in a woman, he sent his mother to talk things over with the woman's mother's sister (her aunt). If everyone agreed, a message was sent to the man's family. The woman didn't have to marry the man if she didn't want to. Then the man had to propose officially. According to one custom, the man would be invited to the woman's house. She would place a bowl of boiled corn outside near the door, then watch. The man would then try to sneak up to the house and eat the corn. If she allowed him to do this, it meant she would marry him. But if she ran out and stopped him, he was out of luck.

If he was accepted, he and his family collected gifts to give to the woman's family. In some tribes, the man had to perform bride service for a year, helping the family and working to prove that he could provide for his future wife. In other tribes, the groom had to build a house and raise a crop to prove he could take care of a family. When he did these things, a marriage ceremony was performed. Once the couple were married, the house and all the property became the wife's.

Although women controlled the wealth and prestige in a tribe, most of the chiefs were men. They were usually the brothers of the most powerful women and from the most important clans in the tribe. The nobles gained power and prestige through the honor of

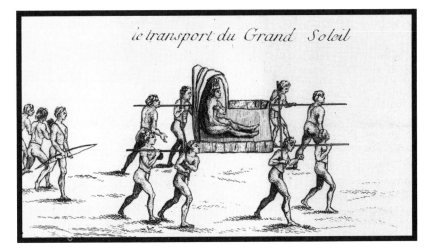

The Great Sun of the Natchez was so revered that his feet were never allowed to touch the ground. He was carried through the town on litters (some covered with flowers) and followed by musicians. He was attended by retainers handpicked by the chief to serve him. *(Hargrett Library, University of Georgia Libraries)*

These two ceremonial flints are part of the Duck River cache, a group of 46 objects accidentally discovered on a Tennessee farm in 1894. These objects, perhaps representing the talons on a bird of prey, were held by a high-ranking official and probably served as symbols of authority. *(Courtesy of the Frank H. McClung Museum, The University of Tennessee, Knoxville)*

their clans, by their age, and partly through their accomplishments as warriors and holy men. The chief and his nobles ran the day-to-day affairs of the village, and some of the largest

Moundbuilder cities had hundreds of nobles who were part of the chief's council.

The chiefs of many towns, especially the largest mound complexes, were revered by the citizens. Chiefs of the village included the war chief, who was responsible for maintaining an army and defending the town, and a peace chief, who handled affairs in the city during times of peace.

In the Grand Village of the Natchez, one of the grandest mound cities in the Southeast, the chief (called the Great Sun) claimed that he was descended from the sun itself. Mallory O'Connor's book, *Lost Cities of the Ancient Southeast,* quotes the following description: "When he dined, the most revered members of the hierarchy sat at his feet, and when he was finished eating, he used his feet to move the bowls in their direction so they could partake of the chiefly repast."

Councils usually met in the chief's council house every day, starting early in the morning. They discussed town affairs, making decisions concerning food distribution, warfare, public-works projects, and other business. Other matters, such as justice or punishment for anyone committing crimes, was the responsibility of the individual clans.

WARFARE

One of the most important decisions a council made was whether to go to war. Most fights were not between tribes but between individual clans within the tribes. Most American Indians believed in a law of retaliation—if a member of one clan was killed, other members of the clan had the right to kill the murderer. Once that death was avenged, there was no more fighting and the matter was settled. Sometimes, though, towns went to war, usually for control of farmland. Occasionally war was waged over trade routes as well. Most warfare only happened in good weather—late spring, summer, and early fall.

When the decision to go to war was made, the entire town prepared for it. Many tribes displayed a red war club in a promi-

This 18-inch-high statue was found in Tennessee and dates to 1400. The English-man John White noticed that among the 16th-century American Indians of coastal Virginia, carved images seemed intended to protect the bodies of their deceased chiefs. This stone image may have served a similar purpose. *(Courtesy of the Frank H. McClung Museum, The University of Tennessee, Knoxville)*

nent place in town and flew a red flag to show that the time for battle was near. The French reported that the Natchez hung their flag from a red war pole that was eight feet long and stuck into the ground so that it pointed in the direction of their enemy.

On the day of combat, the warriors painted their bodies with red and black paint, the symbols for conflict and death, then set out in a group of 20 or 30. According to Charles Hudson's book, *The Southeastern Indians,* "Southeastern warriors traveled almost naked, dressed only in a breechcloth and moccasins. . . . A warrior carried with him a bow and arrows, a knife, and a war club stuck through his belt. Other than this, the warriors carried only a pack containing an old blanket, a small bag of parched corn meal, a wooden cup, perhaps some dried cornbread, and leather and cord to repair their moccasins. . . . They also used armor and shields made of woven cane and bison leather."

Surprise was essential, so the warriors traveled as quietly as they could. Once they got to the enemy village, they usually split into small groups. Each man took care to step in the tracks of the man in front of him, to make it look like only one person was in the forest. If the war party was discovered, they usually went home without fighting. If not, war began.

Most battles were quick and vicious. Many warriors cut off their enemies' heads, then took them home to display on poles outside public buildings. Scalping was also popular. Warriors scalped their enemies by making a cut around the victim's head, placing their feet on the victim's neck, and pulling the scalp off.

Rarely did anyone survive this, but there is at least one example of a woman who was scalped and lived to tell about it. Archaeologists at Moundville—a vast mound city that thrived between A.D. 1000 and 1500—discovered the skull of a young woman that had a shallow groove around the hairline. This groove appeared to be from a knife blade that had cut her. They know that she survived because medical tests discovered that there had been an infection around the wound that eventually healed.

Victorious raiding parties returned to their village with heads, scalps, and sometimes slaves. These slaves were usually given to families who had lost a loved one, and they usually remained with those families the rest of their lives. The entire town celebrated a victory with feasting and storytelling.

EUROPEAN CONTACT

A number of European expeditions penetrated the Southeast in the early 1500s, but few wandered far from the coastlines or the rivers, such as the Mississippi. Then in 1539, Spain sent Hernando De Soto to the New World with instructions to conquer and pacify the land for Spain. He took those orders seriously and proceeded to decimate the peoples he met along the way.

For about three years, from 1539 to 1542, De Soto's expedition roamed the Southeast, beginning in Florida and traveling north, then east, through what is now Georgia, Tennessee, Alabama, Arkansas, and Louisiana. Along the way, he met hundreds of American Indian tribes, some of whom had never before seen a white man. He also found deserted cities that some tribes had fled, fearing the onslaught of the expedition. Some cities were emptied as a result of European diseases that wiped out entire tribes.

De Soto's primary goal was discovering the majestic cities of gold that were rumored to be in the New World. But riches eluded him. Continual battles with Native peoples killed off many men in his expedition, and sickness weakened the group even further. Finally, on May 21, 1542, De Soto died of a fever near southwestern Arkansas. What was left of his expedition floated down the Mississippi on rafts and returned to the Spanish colony of Mexico.

NOTES

p. 40   "[The chief] already had much information . . ." Quoted in David Ewing Duncan, *Hernando DeSoto: A Savage Quest in the Americas* (New York: Crown Publishers, 1995), p. 263.

p. 45   "Because of dislocations . . ." Dr. Brian Butler, associate director/senior scientist, Center for Archaeological Investigations, Southern Illinois University, Carbondale, interview by Allison Lassieur (April 1997).

p. 45   "We really don't have a clue . . ." Dr. Mark Mehrer, archaeologist, Department of Anthropology, Northern Illinois University, De Kalb, interview by Allison Lassieur (April 1997).

p. 46   "We still find domestic houses . . ." Mehrer, interview (April 1997).

p. 47   "They build such sites with the strength of their arms. . . ." Quoted in Robert Silverberg, *The Moundbuilders of Ancient America* (Athens: Ohio University Press, 1968), p. 12.

p. 51   "It had a diameter of more than forty feet. . . ." Peter Nabokov, quoted in Alvin M. Josephy Jr., ed., *America in 1492* (New York: Vintage Books, 1991), p. 138.

p. 51   "We know that people made clay walls . . ." Mehrer, interview (April 1997).

p. 54   "baked either in thin cakes . . ." James Adair, quoted in Duncan, p. 282.

p. 57   "When he dined . . ." Quoted in Mallory O'Connor, *Lost Cities of the Ancient Southeast* (Gainesville: University of Florida Press, 1995), p. 97.

p. 59   "Southeastern warriors traveled almost naked . . ." Charles Hudson, *The Southeastern Indians* (Knoxville: University of Tennessee Press, 1976), p. 247.

KEEPERS OF THE PLAINS

PLAINS PEOPLE

E mpty, vast, inhospitable—no one could possibly have lived in the Great Plains before the coming of the white man. That was the thinking in 1859, when Lewis Henry Morgan, who studied American Indians, said, "The prairie is not congenial to the Indian, and is only made tolerable to him by the possession of the horse and the rifle." Morgan couldn't have been more wrong.

In fact, the prairie lands of the United States were home to American Indians for thousands of years before Europeans arrived. Some Native peoples lived in large, permanent prairie villages surrounded by fields of corn. Others were nomadic, following the buffalo herds on foot. Many tribes combined the two, spending part of the year with the crops and traveling in the summer and fall to hunt buffalo, elk, deer, and other game. But they were definitely there.

Popular images of the Plains Indians comes from television, movies, and the myth of the West—warrior nomads living in tipis and hunting buffalo. This image was perpetuated in the past by archaeologists and historians, who once followed this idea: since buffalo were big and dangerous, the only way they could be hunted was on horseback. Because horses didn't come

Opposite: Before Spanish explorers introduced the horse into Native American culture, most Plains groups lived in small villages, farming the land near rivers and lakes. Nomadic peoples followed the buffalo. After the horse came, many groups abandoned their farms and became full-time buffalo hunters on horseback.

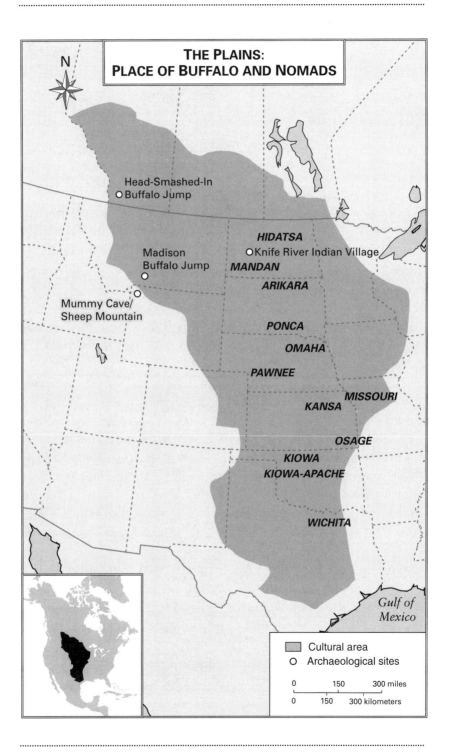

**THE PLAINS:
PLACE OF BUFFALO AND NOMADS**

N

Head-Smashed-In
O Buffalo Jump

Madison
Buffalo Jump

Mummy Cave/
Sheep Mountain

HIDATSA
O Knife River Indian Village
MANDAN

ARIKARA

PONCA

OMAHA

PAWNEE

MISSOURI
KANSA

OSAGE
KIOWA
KIOWA-APACHE

WICHITA

*Gulf of
Mexico*

■ Cultural area
O Archaeological sites

0   150   300 miles
0   150   300 kilometers

to North America until the 1500s,[*] early American Indians couldn't have hunted buffalo. If they did not hunt buffalo, then they could not have lived on the prairie.

The archaeological and historical evidence seemed to follow this reasoning, too. Few artifacts have been found in the Great Plains areas; unlike the rich archaeological sites in the Southeast, the evidence in the Plains is usually limited to scattered camps and small villages. These are tough to find, and until relatively recently few people bothered to look.

Another problem was the ethnographic evidence. After the first wave of European explorers passed through parts of the Great Plains in the 1500s, few others who ventured into the area recorded what they saw. By the time white people began recording the American Indians of the Plains in the early 1800s, most of the tribes had changed and developed into predominantly nomadic peoples. White people thought the Indians had always lived that way and promoted that idea for almost 100 years.

Piece by tiny piece, archaeologists have been reconstructing the real story of life on the Plains before Europeans. They've discovered that large, organized buffalo hunts brought down hundreds of animals without the use of guns or horses. They've found large villages and small camps in places where, a hundred years ago, no scientist would have imagined American Indians had been. They've realized that, far from being the inhospitable place some imagined it to be, the Great Plains provided everything the precontact Native Americans needed to live.

No other area in North America has been as misunderstood as the Great Plains before the coming of the Europeans. To understand the lives of those who lived there, one must remember that there were farms before firearms, permanent houses before horses, and a way of life that bears little resemblance to that of the stereotypical warrior-hunter on horseback.

---

[*]Horses were brought to the North American continent by the Spanish.

LAND

The Great Plains lingers in the minds of most Americans as a sea of golden prairie grasses blowing gently in the wind. This image is true in some places. But for the people who lived on the Plains 500 years ago, it was much more than that. To the east, the Mississippi River winds through meadows and pastures that thrive in the fertile areas near water. The Rocky Mountains pose a majestic barrier to the west. To the south, the grasslands become scrub desert in what is now Texas. The deep forests of present-day south central Canada give the Great Plains its northern boundary.

At first glance, the prairies seem empty. But within this huge area are many kinds of landscapes: dry valleys, fields rich with plants, miles of flatlands, towering mountains, and oceans of prairie grasses. Rivers and streams snake through the flat, feature-less Plains. The impressive-looking Platte River, for example, can be as much as a mile wide and only an inch deep in some places. Others, such as the Rio Grande and the Colorado, are so narrow in some places that it's hard to imagine them as the mighty waterways they are elsewhere. Peter Iversen, in America in 1492, quotes this description: "It is said . . . that [the Plains] has more rivers with less water, and that one can see farther, yet see less, than anywhere in the world."

Plains people also faced living in an area plagued by extreme weather conditions. In some areas of the Great Plains, it could be sunny one day and a blizzard the next. In Nebraska, it's not unusual for winter temperatures to fall well below zero and for summer heat to rise above 100 degrees. Violent storms hit suddenly. On the Plains, there is little shelter from the driving rains in summer and snow in winter.

This combination of climate and landscape had its advantages, however. Hundreds of species of edible plants and grasses grew and thrived in the different areas, giving the people a variety of foods that were unique to the Plains. Game animals thrived on the Plains, including bison, white-tailed deer, mule deer, antelope, mountain goats, bighorn sheep, elk, wolves, bears, and thousands of species of birds and small animals. Even though there were few trees, the Native Americans used the available resources to build houses and create weapons.

In the High Plains, the area of grassy plains east of the Rocky Mountains, buffalo grass and pasture grass covered millions of acres and provided food for the buffalo herds that lived there. Yucca, cactus, and sagebrush thrived in the more southern areas where the prairies turned into desert. In the places where small springs bubbled up from the bedrock, stands of trees flourished, as did wild plants, herbs, and fruits such as berries. In Nebraska, lakes and marshes in the Sandhills provided small game and water birds as well as wild rice. The Plains was, contrary to what Lewis Henry Morgan thought, quite congenial to the people who knew how to live there.

PEOPLE

The people traditionally thought of as Plains Indians—the warriors on horseback with a tipi in the distance—weren't living on the prairie when the first Europeans arrived. The ancestors of many of the tribes known today as Plains tribes were farmers then, living in large agricultural villages on the eastern edges of the prairie. The Mandan, for example, were one of the largest farming tribes of the Plains. They lived in tight communities along the Missouri River in present-day North Dakota. Nearby were the Hidatsa. According to Dean Snow, in his book *The Archaeology of North America*:

> When the first Europeans arrived on the Plains in the six-teenth century, they found agricultural villages confined to the eastern margins. The High Plains had reverted to the foot nomads such as the Kiowa who had been there for mil-lennia, and to newcomers such as the Apache. The Arikara had found their niche alongside the Mandan and Hidatsa. The Pawnee had pulled back to their compact villages nearer the Mississippi, as had the Ponca and Omaha. To the south, the Kansa and Osage, late arrivals from the East-ern forests, joined the others on the Prairie fringe. Still far-ther south, another Plains culture was established by the people we know as the Wichita.

The one thing that characterizes the people of the Plains most is movement. The time before Europeans was full of travel, relocation, and change. Tribes from the northern areas moved south, groups from the arid southern deserts moved north, farmers became nomads, then farmers again, and nomads gave up their lifestyle to settle in river bottoms and grow food. Many people were both farmers and nomads, spending half the year following the bison herds, then returning in the fall to harvest the crops and settle in for the winter. Archaeologists find village remains hundreds of miles apart that include artifacts made by the same group of people. Native American myths and stories detail how some tribes moved from place to place.

Why was there so much movement? One theory is that some huge climate change severely affected the people. According to the archaeological record, beginning in 1470 a series of droughts ravaged most of the Plains areas. The droughts lasted more than 40 years and at first only affected the agricultural communities in the High Plains. But as the droughts wore on, the vast farmlands of the eastern Plains were affected. Today, archaeologists think that hundreds of villages were abandoned, tribes moved great distances to find a better life, and the landscape of many areas was permanently changed. Scattered tribes joined forces and established new, tightly knit communities.

VILLAGES

Each tribe, from the sedentary eastern farmers to the High Plains nomads, maintained a distinct way of living. Archaeologist Dr. Michael Fosha of the South Dakota Archaeological Research Center explains, "Each population has their own ideas of what a house is. They already know in their minds, it's a blending of culture and necessity. They use the earth and grass because that's what they have. But there's a lot more to it. Their culture dictates what those things should look like—what grass would repel water best, what types of earth they would use that would survive winter and

Beautifully made pottery was a hallmark of the Pawnee. These pots were found in Nebraska. *(NebraskaLand Magazine/Nebraska Game and Parks Commission)*

spring better than others." The Mandan's villages tended to be built on terraces or bluffs overlooking the Missouri River. This was as much for protection as it was for access to good farmlands. The steep riverbanks offered a barrier against attack on one side, and high palisades encircled the rest of the village. Surrounding that were defensive ditches, usually 10 to 15 feet wide.

A central plaza where ceremonies and games were held dominated the village. It was also the place where people gathered to discuss news, to gossip, and to visit with their friends and family. In some villages, the houses were built in streets surrounding the plaza, but in others the houses were clustered in groups around the plaza. In the mid-1800s, an artist named George Catlin painted dozens of pictures of Mandan villages and life. Evidence that scientists find today matches the paintings so well that many believe the Mandan had lived the same way for hundreds of years—long before whites came.

Catlin painted many Mandan earth lodges. Each lodge was circular, usually between 40 and 80 feet around, with a floor that was about two feet below the ground. Archaeologist Ned Hennenburger of the South Dakota Research Archaeological Research Center observes, "They would start by either removing the sod or excavating a shallow basin upon which they would build their structure. Then they'd go out and cut timbers and set these around the perimeter, like studs." Then four posts were set up in the middle, and cross beams were laid from these posts to the outer ring of studs. These beams were left open for a smoke hole. A thick layer of willow branches, grasses, and matting were laid on top of these beams, and then the whole thing was covered with more earth.

Dr. Fosha explains, "When we excavate a burned house that had grass woven in the rafters and the walls before the earth was packed on, we're left with piles of silicon. It looks like fried glass. It is the cell

This Pawnee pot was decorated by cutting a design in the wet clay before it was fired. Pots like this one were shaped with a grooved paddle made from a buffalo vertebral spine. It has been decorated with a carved human figure. *(Nebraska Land Magazine/ Nebraska Game and Parks Commission)*

TREASURE UNDERFOOT

When an archaeologist gets to a site, it doesn't look like much to the untrained eye. But small clues tell what lies beneath the dirt. These illustrations show the stages of life of a prehistoric Plains house site, from the time it was inhabited to the moment archaeologists find it 400 years later.

1. House site, 1500
This drawing shows what a typical precontact Plains house might have looked like. The lodge is dug partway into the earth, with a thatch roof made of wooden beams and grasses. Surrounding the house at ground level is a berm, which is a ridge of dirt piled on the sides of the house. It was dug when the floor was made. In the floor of the house is a food-storage pit, and there is another pit right outside the doorway.

2. House site, 1650
A hundred and fifty years after the house was abandoned, not much is left. The berms are still here, but they're much smaller. They outline the shape of the house and show how large it was at one time. The pit where the house was is mostly filled in with dirt and debris, as is the storage pit outside. Nothing is left of the roof or building materials used to construct the house. There may be post holes in the ground to show where the wall supports once stood. The surrounding land is beginning to cover the site.

3. House site, 20th century
When an archaeologist finds a site, it's usually in the middle of a farmer's field. This makes sense, because Native Americans built their villages near good farmlands. There's usually a layer of plowed dirt over everything. The archaeologist digs through this to find the house. The remains of the two storage pits still exist. A few post holes also survived. By now, there's nothing left of the berms or the pit of the house itself.

walls of the grasses that burned in an environment where air couldn't get to them, and they just turned to silicon. That's one way archaeologists can tell what a house was made of."

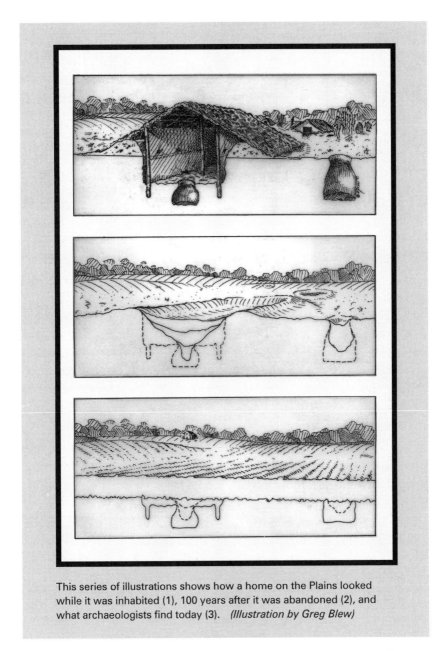

This series of illustrations shows how a home on the Plains looked while it was inhabited (1), 100 years after it was abandoned (2), and what archaeologists find today (3). *(Illustration by Greg Blew)*

The thick walls of an earth lodge provided excellent insulation, keeping it cool in summer and warm in winter. People slept on boxlike rawhide beds that were built on a platform around the inside walls. They kept food and personal belongings in storage areas behind the beds. Archaeologists sometimes find that the floor was honeycombed with deep pits, lined with dried grass and used to store corn and other vegetables. When the food rotted or the grass got wet, the pit was turned into a trash pit.

On the right side of the lodge, ceremonial bundles and weapons were stored. In the center, the women cooked the meals in winter. Summer cooking was done outdoors. Between the fire and the doorway, couches made of bison furs with willow backrests sat on the floor. Important guests and the older men in the family sat here. Some houses were so large that they even had an area to one side of the doorway where horses were kept during cold weather.

In the winter, family members spent their time inside the lodge making tools, pottery, and other objects. With people everywhere, they occasionally dropped things or left some trash behind. This debris is what tells archaeologists about the people's lives. Dr. Fosha says, "When you excavate a site, you can see thousands of human events that took place. Sometimes you find a pile of flint chips where they were either refurbishing or making tools, like a work station. That is quite common. Hearths, with a lot of broken, charred bones are where they prepared food."

The Wichita, who lived on the southern plains, built thatched houses instead of earth lodges. They were primarily a farming people who originally lived in what is now Arkansas and Oklahoma before migrating north. Their villages were fairly large, some covering as much as 100 acres. Rather than building a palisaded village, the Wichita built their houses in a tight knot in the center of their fields, with crops radiating out from the village like spokes in a wheel.

The houses that the nomadic tribes lived in are harder to reconstruct. Unlike the inhabitants of fortified, populated villages, who left many traces, the nomadic tribes rarely stayed in one place long enough to leave much behind. Flint chips, charred bones from a cooking fire, a ring of rocks that held down a tipi, or the cleaned bones from their successful hunts are sometimes all that are left.

Scattered throughout remote places in the Plains are small wooden structures, badly deteriorated but still recognizable even today. Amazingly, these houses, built hundreds of years ago, managed to survive wind, weather, and the encroachment of Europeans. These time capsules of precontact life are precious to archaeologists. Some consist of only a few poles leaning against a rock outcropping. Others are more elaborate, such as a tipi-shaped lodge made of wooden poles in northwest Wyoming. A few of them were built by the earliest nomadic Plains peoples hundreds of years before contact. Although archaeologists find arrowheads, weapon fragments, and animal bones at these sites, these discoveries tell little about who the people were or exactly how they lived.

FOOD

Although bison meat provided a large part of the food for the Plains tribes, the people did not live on buffalo alone. Most tribes relied on their fields of beans, corn, and squash for much of their diet. Drawings made by European explorers show rich fields full of food. Plains farmers did not cultivate massive fields for hundreds of people, as did the farmers of the Woodlands or the people in the Moundbuilding South. They made do with smaller fields, a shorter growing season, and a variety of plants that could withstand the extreme weather conditions of the Plains.

Most crops were grown in the dark soils near rivers and streams. The Mandan, Hidatsa, and Crow made their homes in areas where loose river soil, continually replenished by flooding, was plentiful. This kind of soil was good for planting because it was easy to dig, unlike the tough sod of the prairie lands. Lands near rivers and other water sources were also less likely to dry up in the hot prairie summers. If the summer was especially dry, it wasn't too difficult to carry water to the fields.

Women were responsible for planting and cultivating the crops. They owned the land and all the produce that came from it, and it was their right to distribute it to members of their families.

Baskets like these were used to collect and store seeds. These three baskets were made by people in the Pai communities along the Colorado River. *(The Field Museum, Chicago, Neg #A 107735a)*

Each plot, more like a large garden than a true farm field, was owned by one extended family. During the busiest times of the growing season, everyone in the family pitched in to help.

In the fall, the men cleared new lands by cutting the brush and timber so that everything fell in one direction. According to Robert Spencer, in *The Native Americans*, "Some of the timber that was fit might be taken home for firewood; the rest was left to dry until spring. The object of felling the trees in one direction was to make them cover the ground as much as possible, since burning them softened the soil and left it loose and mellow for planting."

In spring, as soon as the last frosts left the prairie, planting began. Each field was usually rectangular, five or six acres, and most of it was devoted to maize. Maize was planted in little mounds spaced about four feet apart. A woman slowly planted six to eight seeds in each mound by pressing them into the earth with her thumb. Beans were planted in the ground between the mounds. In the Northeast squash, the third "sister" of the Eastern Woodland farmers, was grown separately, in an area where the growing corn plants wouldn't shade it too much. Along the edges of the fields, the women planted sunflowers and pumpkins.

As soon as the crops were planted, platforms were built in the fields. Women and children stayed there during the day, keeping the fields weeded and guarding the young plants from birds and deer.

As the corn grew, fresh green ears were picked, boiled, and eaten. Trash pits that archaeologists excavate are filled with the remains of all this corn. Green corn was picked regularly, and new corn was planted in its place to keep the supply coming for as long as the weather permitted. Most of the corn was left to ripen completely before it was picked, however. At the end of the harvesting time, the village had a feast in the middle of the fields to celebrate.

Some of the corn was dried for seed, some was saved for trade. But most of it was dried, put into containers, and stored in pits. Squash was picked, cut into squares, and strung on long poles to dry in the sun. The dried squash kept for months without spoiling and was cooked with cornmeal and meat. Pieces of dried corn and squash, sometimes found at a dig site, tell scientists exactly what the people ate.

Not every Great Plains farming community relied so heavily on corn, however. The Hidatsa had never eaten corn before they migrated west and met the Mandan. According to legend, it was the Mandan who introduced them to corn. They liked the taste and began growing it themselves. But beans were the staple food of the Hidatsa, and they grew five different kinds. "They called them ama'ca ci'pica (black bean), ama'ca hi'ci (red bean), ama'ca pu'xi (spotted bean), ama'ca ita wina'ki matu'hica (shield-figured bean), and ama'ca ata'ki (white bean)," quotes Peter Iversen in *America in 1492*.

The crops that the Pawnee grew were closely tied to their religious beliefs, and they grew more kinds of vegetables than most of the other Plains farmers. They filled their fields with 10 types of corn, eight kinds of beans, and seven varieties of squash and pumpkins. Each vegetable had its own meaning and ritual.

For example, the Pawnee considered one kind of corn to be holy and grew it only for religious purposes. They wrapped an ear in buffalo skin for winter, and another for summer. They then ceremoniously planted this corn to ensure good harvests.

As soon as the crops were planted, it was time for the summer buffalo hunt. In most villages, some people stayed behind to tend the fields while the rest packed their belongings and prepared to follow the herds. They stayed on the move for months, camping in prime hunting areas for a few weeks, then moving on as the herds migrated across the Plains in search of food and water.

It took a lot of skill (and some luck) to bring down buffalo, and buffalo hunters were masters in how to outsmart their prey. The hunters knew when and where the herds traveled and planned the hunt carefully each season. First, they set up camp near the base of a particular cliff. This camp would serve as both a home during the hunt and a buffalo-processing facility once the animals were killed.

The men piled brush and rocks, called "dead men," along a specific route that led to the cliff's edge high above. These piles were formed in a triangular corridor, with the fence becoming narrower as it got closer to the cliff's edge. Some of these ancient traps are still set up on remote cliffs. Archaeologists can see exactly how the hunters constructed them and guess how many buffalo one could ensnare.

Once the trap was ready, the hunters waited. Soon the herd passed by. Bison herds are usually led by a mature cow, and the hunters used this fact to their advantage. One man disguised himself in a wolf or coyote skin while another covered himself with a robe made of a bison calf. The "wolf" pretended to attack the "calf," which caused the cow to move and protect the baby. The hunters were able to direct the herd into the trap and stampede them over the cliff. In the 19th century, European explorers recorded this, and artists such as George Catlin painted images of hunters wrapped in skins, stalking their prey.

Hundreds of bison fell to their death. A group of hunters was usually stationed at the bottom of the cliff, armed with bows and

THE MANY USES FOR
A BUFFALO SKIN

Buffalo provided much more than food for the Plains peoples.
Buffalo skins with the hair left on became warm winter cloaks.
The hair was removed to make light summer blankets or soft
leather for shoes and clothing. Other skins, tanned and
stretched, made coverings for the lodges. The thick hide of a
buffalo's neck was ideal for making tough war shields that
could withstand arrows. Untanned hides were made into ket-
tles for boiling meat. Cut strips of hide were braided into ropes
and strings, and buffalo hair made wonderful stuffing for cush-
ions and bedding. The men carved dishes and spoons from the
horns. Hooves were boiled to make glue that the hunters used
to attach arrowheads and flèches. Ribs were turned into hide
scrapers and runners for small sleds pulled by dogs. Shoulder
blades became farming tools such as hoes and fleshers. And
the tail, lashed to a stick, became a fly brush.

arrows. Any animal that survived the fall was shot immediately.
When the last animals had been driven over the cliffs, the women
began their job of preparing the carcasses.

The camp became a factory of buffalo processing, lasting until
every animal was butchered. Most of the meat was dried on huge
wooden racks left in the sun. The dried meat was then ground into
mush and mixed with buffalo fat and wild berries to make pem-
mican, a staple of Plains life. The mix was placed in an airtight
skin bag and would keep for months. Grease was extracted from
bones through boiling. In *Prehistoric Hunters of the High Plains*,
George C. Frison quotes the following description: "Stone boiling
pits were lined with a green bison hide, then filled with water,
broken bones, and hot stones. [The hot stones boiled the water],
and the boiling water released grease from the bone. The grease
was skimmed off as it floated to the top."

Today, archaeologists find enormous masses of buffalo bones
beneath some cliffs in the Plains. The bones tell the story of how
people processed the meat. Piles of bones were organized by body

part, leg bones in one place, skulls in another. The remains of boiling pits, along with thousands of fragments of boiling stones, tell scientists that these people were serious and thorough about their work.

When all the work was done, the camp packed up and moved to a new buffalo jump site. By the end of the summer most hunting parties returned to the village laden with meat and supplies. The meat, combined with the crops and the wild berries, seeds, and plants that were collected throughout the summer, provided the village enough food to last through the winter.

SOCIETY

Little is known about the societies of the precontact nomadic tribes because few records exist today. Archaeologists know more about the farming communities, especially the Mandan and the Hidatsa, from both the archaeological record and the writings of early explorers who lived with and studied the tribes.

Like most of the North American tribes before contact, the Mandan were a matrilineal society. Descent was traced through the women in a group, and women controlled the land and most of the food supply. Each family worked a parcel of land as long as there were enough women in the family to care for it. If for some reason the family got smaller or no girls were born, it would give some of its land to other families.

When two people got married, they lived with the woman's mother and her female relatives in one lodge. A single lodge might hold a family of 30 or 40 people, related through the women in the clan. All the children of a marriage belonged to the woman's clan and were not seen as related to their father. The father's role was to raise his sister's children, with whom he shared a lineage.

The Hidatsa and the Crow followed this system as well. The Crow eventually became a nomadic tribe, but since it had once been part of the Hidatsa, it kept its matrilineal traditions. Crow men moved into the women's houses after marriage, and all the men living in one clan house tended to hunt and socialize together.

Although most of Mandan daily life was influenced by the women, the tribal councils were headed by men. The Mandan council consisted of the older males, and they regularly met to discuss the business of the tribe. They made decisions by persuading others rather than by voting and arguments. In this way, the council could come to a consensus without fighting.

EUROPEAN CONTACT

The first contact with Europeans in the Plains was an indirect one: the arrival of horses. In the mid-1500s, long before many Native Americans saw their first European, horses from Spanish expeditions in the Southwest escaped and were taken by local tribes. Soon people throughout North America were trading and breeding these new animals. In less than 100 years, the horse completely changed the Plains way of life.

Agricultural tribes, such as the Crow, abandoned their farms and became full-time nomads. The Hidatsa gave up their bison hunting and became full-time farmers. The Arikara, who had been farmers for hundreds of years, became nomads but maintained their farming villages. Entire tribes moved to different areas of the Plains, and some eastern groups—pushed out of the Eastern Woodlands by European colonization and warfare—migrated to the Plains.

Although a few fur trappers and explorers visited the Plains in the 1700s, it was the Lewis and Clark expedition of 1804 to 1806 that made the first contact with many of the Plains tribes. On this expedition, the duo journeyed from the Pacific and recorded many of the Native Americans they encountered. The Mandans and Hidatsa welcomed the expedition into their villages in the winter of 1804–1805, little realizing that this was but the first drop in a flood that would destroy them in less than 80 years.

WE DO NOT WANT
YOUR PRESENTS

The Pawnee, a hunting and farming people, lived in large earth-lodge villages along the Platte River in Nebraska—right in the path of westward-moving settlers. At a treaty session between the Pawnee and the whites, Curly Chief recounted a Pawnee's rejection of European goods. Although there is no record of when he said this, Curly Chief spoke for Plains people from all times when he uttered these words.

> There was a time when there were no people in this country except Indians. After that, the people began to hear of men that had white skins; they had been seen far to the east. Before I was born they came to our country. The man who came was from the Government. He wanted to make a treaty with us and to give us presents, blankets, guns, flint, steel, and knives. The Head Chief told him we needed none of these things. . . . He said, "You see, my brother, that the Ruler has given us all that we need; the buffalo for food and clothing; the corn to eat with our dried meat, bows, arrows, knives, and hoes; all the implements we need for killing meat or for cultivating the ground. Now go back to the country from whence you came. We do not want your presents and we do not want you to come into our country."

NOTES

p. 62   "The prairie is not congenial . . ." Quoted in Philip Kopper, *The Smithsonian Book of North American Indians Before the Coming of the Europeans* (Washington D.C.: Smithsonian Books, 1986), p. 169.

p. 65   "It is said . . ." Peter Iversen, quoted in Alvin M. Josephy Jr., ed., *America in 1492* (New York: Vintage Books, 1991), p. 87.

p. 66   "When the first Europeans arrived . . ." Dean Snow, *The Archaeology of North America* (London: Thames and Hudson, 1976), p. 91.

pp. 67–68 "Each population had their own ideas . . ." Dr. Michael Fosha, archaeologist, South Dakota Archaeological Research Center, Rapid City, interview by Allison Lassieur (April 1997).

p. 69   "They would start by either removing . . ." Dr. Ned Hennen-
               burger, archaeologist, South Dakota Archaeological Research
               Center, Rapid City,   interview by Allison Lassieur (April
               1997).

pp. 69–70 "When we excavate a burned house . . ." Fosha, interview
               (April 1997).

p. 72   "When you excavate a site . . ." Fosha, interview (April 1997).

p. 74   "Some of the timber that was fit . . ." Robert F. Spencer, *The
               Native Americans: Ethnology and Backgrounds of the North
               American Indians* (New York: Harper & Row, 1977), p. 320.

p. 75   "They called them . . ." Iversen, quoted in Josephy, p. 94.

p. 77   "Stone boiling pits were lined . . ." Quoted in George C. Fri-
               son, *Prehistoric Hunters of the High Plains* (New York: Harcourt
               Brace Jovanovich, 1991), p. 216.

p. 80   "There was a time . . ." Curly Chief, quoted in Peter Nabokov,
               Native American Testimony (New York: Viking Penguin, 1978),
               p. 39.

SPIRITS OF THE DESERT

PEOPLE OF THE SOUTHWEST

In the winter of 1888, two cowboys, Richard Wetherill and Charlie Mason, wandered slowly through snow-dusted Colorado scrub looking for lost cattle. They were just about ready to return home when one of them, spying a strange shadow under an outcropping of rock far above them, shouted for his companion.

Thanks to a few lost cattle, these two men stumbled upon a great adobe (mud brick) dwelling, nestled under a huge cliff. This chance discovery was met with excitement and endless speculation in the archaeological community. Who built this place? Why? How was it constructed? And most important, why was it abandoned?

In the years since this discovery, archaeologists and historians have crawled all over this site, seeking answers within its silent, crumbling walls. Now called Cliff Palace, this dwelling was built by an ancient tribe of the Southwest peoples known as the Anasazi (Ancient Ones). Decades of research have told how they lived, what they ate, and myriad details about their daily lives. By the 1300s—more than 200 years before the first Europeans came to the Southwest in search of gold—Cliff Palace and hundreds of other magnificent adobe dwellings like it lay abandoned and open to slow ruin.

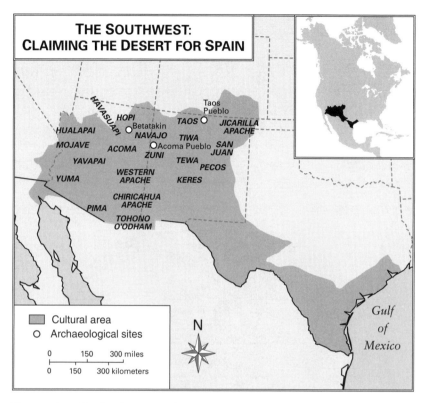

The people of the Southwest developed complex irrigation systems to water their fields in the dry desert lands. At the time that Spanish explorers invaded their lands in the mid-1500s, the people had cultivated huge areas and had built vast cities of adobe structures that reached up to five stories high.

Interestingly, a lot of archaeological investigation stopped there. The 200 plus years between the fall of the Ancient Ones and the arrival of the first Spanish expeditions in the Southwest seems to have been all but ignored. Books go on for hundreds of pages about the Anasazi, only to trail off with vague paragraphs about what might have happened after their demise. It's almost as if the people of the ancient pueblos (cities made of adobe) vanished, only to appear again in time for the Spanish to meet them a few hundred years later.

Of course, this isn't true. During of this "empty" time between 1300 and 1540, immense changes swept through the Southwest.

The inhabitants of entire cities migrated to other areas, tribes broke from one another and formed new societies, warfare decimated some peoples, and strangers from the far north gradually settled in the area. Sedentary farmers relied on thousands of years of accumulated knowledge of agriculture to coax crops from the hard, sunbaked soil. Others maintained a nomadic existence, traveling from place to place with the seasons to hunt and gather food. Large adobe cities grew, flourished, and died, only to be reestablished somewhere else. Complex trade routes crisscrossed

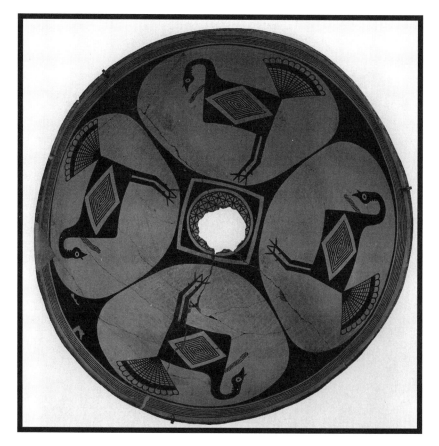

About 500 years before European contact, the Mongolon peoples of the Mimbres area in the Southwest created striking pottery such as this turkey bowl. The Zuni are descended from these skilled craftspeople. *(Peabody Museum, Harvard University/photo by Hillel Burger)*

the desert, leading to places as far away as the Pacific Ocean to the west and the lush forests of the Southeast.

But the people who met the Europeans in the 1500s were linked to the mysterious Ancient Ones of the past. "Their village architecture, their splendid turquoise jewelry, and their stunning geometric black-and-white pottery eventually became part of Pueblo Indian culture. . . . Whatever caused the depopulation of the Anasazi communities reinforced a guiding principle . . . that life was fragile, and harmony difficult to achieve and maintain," quotes Alvin M. Josephy Jr. in *America in 1492*.

LAND

In many places, the Southwest lives up to its reputation as a stark, hostile place. But the Southwest is also a place of incredible beauty. In New Mexico, towers of stone in Monument Valley seem to stand guard over hundreds of miles of desert. A cool, blue-green waterfall in Havasu Canyon in Colorado gave the Havasupai people their name. From the lush mountain grasslands of the Navajo homes on the Kaibab Plateau to the pink-orange sandstone mesas of the Hopi, the variety of the landscape and climate of the Southwest has defined and nourished the cultures who have lived there.

Today, the Southwest includes northern New Mexico, Arizona, parts of Utah and Colorado, and a sliver of Mexico. The Southwest can be divided into three kinds of environments: high plateaus in the north, hot deserts in the south, and a spine of mountains in the central region between. The weather and temperature of each place vary greatly, depending on its altitude. For example, in Yuma, Arizona, the lowest and driest point in the Southwest, the average temperature is 72 degrees Fahrenheit. Travel to Flagstaff, a few hundred miles northeast, and its average temperature drops almost 30 degrees—to a cool 45 degrees Fahrenheit.

In plateau country, the Colorado and San Juan Rivers wind through colorful, high-topped mesas and deep canyons, including the Grand Canyon. Forests of yellow pines, piñons, and junipers live in the higher elevations; sagebrush and other desert plants live lower. Thunderstorms are quick and violent here, blowing in without warning and unleashing a downpour in minutes.

The rugged mountain ranges of the central region stay cool throughout most of the year, providing a welcome respite from the hot desert summers. Pine forests blanket much of the mountains, and streams flow through deep mountain valleys and pastures teeming with plants and wildlife.

In each region, the people used the variations of the land to their advantage. They planted their crops in the fertile areas, then traveled to the higher elevations to gather nuts, berries, and other plant life. They traveled with the seasons but always returned to their pueblo homes.

PEOPLE

The Southwest before the arrival of the Europeans was home to many distinctive American Indian cultures. The farmers and hunters of the river valleys included the Yuma, Mojave, Havasupai, Walapai, Pima, and Yaqui. Some tribes, such as the Pima, settled in the river valleys of the Colorado, Gila, and Rio Grande and planted large crops beside the rivers. Others were what some archaeologists call "part farmers." They planted where they could but also relied heavily on hunting for food.

From spring until fall each year, the Havasupai lived—as they still do today—in the fertile depths of the Grand Canyon. Havasu Falls, which plummets into a sparkling blue-green pool, gave the Havasupai their name: "People of the Blue-Green Water." The Walapai, whose name means "Pine Tree People," lived south of the Grand Canyon and relied on hunting for their livelihood. The "People of the Sun," the Yavapai, ranged throughout Arizona.

The Navajo and Apache peoples are not originally from the Southwest, although they are indelibly linked with the region. Robert F. Spencer, in his book *The Native Americans*, explains, "The precise time of arrival of the Navajo and . . . the Apache in the Southwest is still shrouded in mysteries which the archaeologists

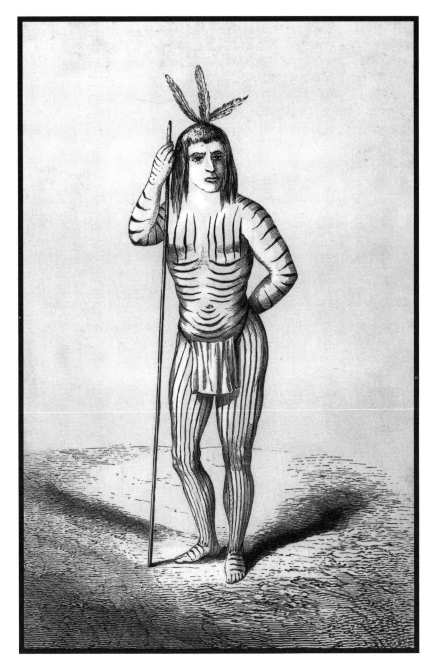

This Mojave man stands proudly with his spear and body paint. The Mojave were expert hunters and farmers. *(Photo courtesy of the Newberry Library, Chicago)*

The precontact Southwest peoples grew cotton and wove it into clothing such as this shirt. Much of the cloth they made is known for its complex designs and its lacy look. *(Arizona State Museum, University of Arizona)*

have been unable to penetrate, although it is generally conceded that [they] have been in the region for at least 400 or 500 years." Sometime in the 1300s, around the same time that the Anasazi were abandoning their cliff dwellings, the Navajo and the Apache were slowly moving southward from northern Canada. They were nomadic hunters when they arrived, but they learned how to farm from the people who lived here.

In northern New Mexico and Arizona, pueblo villages were home to thousands of people. Documents that survive from European exploration describe these vast cities. Descendants of the Anasazi, these cultures still live in the areas once inhabited by their ancestors. The eastern pueblo tribes, including the Keres, Tiwa, Tewa, and Towa, built their villages near the fertile lands of the Rio Grande. The western groups—including the Zuni and Hopi—relied on sporadic seasonal rains and the runoff for their crops. These groups planted their corn at the mouths of washes to ensure that enough water would run into them for a successful growing season.

The one thing that all these people had in common was their respect for the land and what it gave to them. Water was precious, life was fragile, and they lived in balance with the resources of their world.

VILLAGES

No other region of North America had so many different kinds of villages and ways of life within its borders. Some cultures carried on the traditions of those who came before them. Others built on their knowledge by adding new ideas and creating a distinct way of living.

The Yuma lived in sprawling villages near the fertile river lands of the lower Colorado. Houses were separated by huge fields, and one village could stretch for miles along a river. In the winter, the Yuma lived in rectangular earth houses. For warm weather, they built open platforms roofed with branches to stay cool.

For the farming Pima and Tohono O'odham (also called Papago) tribes, village life was more complicated. The desert where they lived was one of the hottest and driest areas of the Southwest, so they had to move frequently to follow the water in different seasons. In the summer, they lived in field villages built near their crops. Each family built a roof on four posts without walls where they cooked meals and slept. When winter came, the tribe moved into their villages in the mountains. Their winter houses were large, round buildings with flat tops made of grasses and covered with earth.

When the Navajo first arrived in the Southwest in the 1300s, they were a warrior people. They built their villages on high bluffs, ridges, and mesas that could be easily defended. Later, as they adapted farming skills from other tribes, they gradually became agriculturalists. They lived in round houses with conical roofs, called hogans. According to Robert F. Spencer, "The pile stick hogan has a foundation of three upright forked cedar poles locked together at the apex. Additional logs are leaned together over this foundation, and the whole is plastered over with mud and earth." Inside, the family slept on mattresses made of boughs and animal skins arranged around a central fire. Baskets of personal belongings lined the walls, and food and other belongings hung from the rafters above.

For the Apache, life in this new land was full of change. They began as nomads, traveling great distances to hunt and fight. Soon they settled in permanent villages and began farming. The Apache borrowed ideas about house construction from their pueblo-dwelling neighbors and built towns of large adobe houses. The earliest Apache houses in the Southwest were built in the 1500s, just before the Spanish explorers arrived. Their villages, located near good farmlands, served as a home base when they traveled to hunt.

Archaeologists have unearthed the remains of houses they think were built by the Apache. All that's left now are foundations and a few fire pits, but they tell much about the families that once lived there. Each house was divided into rooms. Some served as kitchens, where most of the cooking was done. A D-shaped fire pit was built against one wall, leaving the room clear for food preparation. Other rooms had fire pits, and they were probably used to heat the house during cool weather.

Outside, near the house, a bell-shaped baking pit served to cook breads and other baked goods for the family.

The Apache lived relatively peacefully in these villages, hunting and farming, until the horse came to the Southwest.

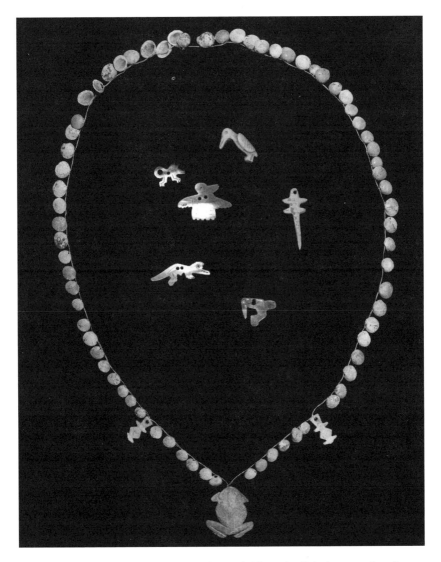

The Pima and the Tohono O'odham are descended from the Hohokam peoples of southern Arizona. This exquisite jewelry, made of shells and carved bone, were found at the Hohokam city of Snaketown. *(Arizona State Museum, University of Arizona)*

With horses, they abandoned their villages and became nomads again, using the newly acquired animal to travel wherever hunting was good.

The pueblo villages were by far the most rich and complex communities of the Southwest. When the Spanish first came to the area in the mid-1500s, there were more than 80 pueblo villages throughout the Southwest. They were home to thousands of people, including the Hopi, Zuni, Keres, Tewa, and many others. Spencer continues, "Before the arrival of the Spanish there had been an even greater shrinkage of the number of towns, with the depopulation of literally hundreds of pueblos. Prolonged drought conditions account for this in part; when water supplies fail, people must migrate. Other villages were probably abandoned [because of] raiders such as the Ute and Comanche."

The basic pueblo village of the precontact peoples is little changed from the pueblos of today: apartment-like adobe structures housing several families. But they are more than buildings. The closeness to the land that the pueblo-dwelling peoples have is reflected in their homes, and each tribe had its distinctive style that makes its village uniquely its own.

More than 6,000 people lived in the grand Acoma pueblo, which is one of the oldest continually inhabited sites in North America. The pueblo was built near lands where maize, squash, and beans would grow. On top of the pueblo, huge cisterns caught rainwater for drinking. Several plazas within the village were connected by streets. A maze of underground tunnels beneath the streets helped the people of Acoma escape to their homes during battle.

Captain Hernando de Alvarado, a member of Spanish explorer Francisco de Coronado's 1540 expedition into the Southwest, described a smaller Keres village he saw:

> The village was up on a rock out of reach, having steep
> sides in every direction. . . . There was a broad stairway
> of about 200 steps, then a stretch of about 100 narrower
> steps and at the top they had to go up by means of holes

in the rock, in which they put the points of their feet, holding on at the same time by their hands. There was a wall of large and small stones at the top, which they could roll down without showing themselves, so that no army could possibly be strong enough to capture the village. On the top they had room to sow and store a large amount of corn, and cisterns to collect snow and water.

The Zuni pueblo villages were compact, with narrow streets that led to plazas scattered in different neighborhoods. Multistoried apartment buildings lined the streets and the plazas. There were no stairways to the upper floors; the people used ladders that leaned against the sides of the buildings to get to small trapdoors in the roofs.

Inside, small windows were covered with slabs of a mineral called selenite, which was semitranslucent and let in light. Low built-in benches lined the walls. The whole family slept on blankets and skins spread on the floors. In some rooms, families hung a pole from the rafters, much like a closet rack, where they hung their clothing, extra blankets, and other items. Precious ceremonial garments and objects were carefully stored in a dark interior room, away from the bustle of everyday life.

Corner fireplaces in many rooms heated the apartment in winter. The thick adobe walls also kept the interiors very cool during the hot desert summers. Small wall niches, which looked like windows that had been sealed over, served as storage areas where small objects and some food were kept.

In the living area, every house had a milling box for grinding corn. These long adobe boxes, open on the side facing the room, were divided into three compartments. In each one was a large stone used for grinding corn. Women sat at these boxes and ground corn, talking and enjoying one another's company while they worked. "Five or six women together grind raw corn in a single mill, and from this flour they make many different kinds of bread," quotes Herbert Eugene Bolton in his book, *Spanish Exploration in the Southwest 1542–1706.*

Many of the cultures who lived in the Southwest before the Europeans are gone, and their villages and ways of life gone with them. Others, such as the Hopi and Zuni, and those at Acoma, have survived and flourished. Little archaeological evidence of the departed tribes remains. Archaeologists rely on the accounts of early explorers for information about many of the Southwest tribes, then use the information to find the remains of these once great cultures.

FOOD

The Southwest peoples were, and are today, a desert culture. Many days, they awoke to clear skies, blistering heat, parched land, and fields always in need of water. Only in the river valleys near the great Colorado, Salt, and Rio Grande could anyone feel secure about having water—and even then, drought was always a threat.

The Pueblo peoples mastered the art and science of growing crops in the southwestern soil. Everywhere in the Southwest, from the arid desert to the high mountains, corn was the food crop of choice. Numerous Europeans wrote of the farmed fields, and they were amazed that people could grow anything in such inhospitable places. But the location for each field was chosen very carefully, based on how easily water could get to it. Some tribes planted their fields on high mesas. Others chose places where irrigation ditches could be the most useful. Some tribes, such as the Tohono O'odham, practiced "flash flood" farming. They planted their crops in valleys where the arroyos (washes) fanned out and flooded the area when the rains finally came.

Along with corn, most people planted squash, beans, gourds, cotton, and tobacco. Because the Tohono O'odham depended so heavily on beans in their diet, especially during lean years, early explorers sometimes called them Papago, or "Bean People." Different tribes grew other vegetables, such as pumpkins, depending on where they lived and how long the growing season was. Bolton quotes, "They have fields of maize, beans, and gourds in large quantities. Some of the fields are under irrigation, possessing very good diverting ditches, while others are dependent upon the weather."

Although the cultures of the Southwest were matrilineal (women owned the crops and most of the property in a family), in some tribes it was the men who planted and cultivated. Each family was responsible for its own fields, and kinspeople in a family usually worked together. In the spring, before planting, Zuni men cleared their fields by burning the brush and breaking up the soil. Then they dug irrigation ditches from the water source—either an arroyo or a river—to the fields. Dams or ditches around the fields held the water in, keeping it from running off when the rains came.

May was planting time. The men molded small earth mounds, about six feet apart, throughout the fields. With their digging sticks, they poked holes in these mounds and dropped in the seeds, then covered the holes with earth. After the crops were planted, the men built a wooden windbreak around the fields to protect the young plants from the strong desert winds.

During the growing season, workers guarded the crops from birds and animals and weeded the fields with hoes made from wood and animal bones. Bolton continues to quote, "Each one has in his field a canopy with four stakes and covered on top, where they take him food daily at noon and where he takes his siesta, for ordinarily they are in their fields from morning until night."

The first frost, usually in September or October, meant it was time for the harvest. Everyone in the family helped pick the corn, which was shucked and dried in the sun on the pueblo roofs. After the corn dried, it was stored in large ceramic jars and baskets inside the coolest rooms in the center of the houses, where it stayed until it was ground into flour.

While the men worked in the fields, the women spent their days collecting plant foods. Tohono O'odham women gathered grass seeds, mesquite beans, and, in lean times, fruits from yucca and cactus plants. Large groves of piñon trees provided many tribes with nuts, which were ground and used as flour to make breads and stews. Many tribes also gathered wild rice, walnuts, acorns, and sunflower seeds. The Tohono O'odham harvested the sweet fruit of the giant saguaro cactus and ate it fresh, dried into candy, or boiled into a syrup.

All Southwest tribes hunted, and many villages left their homes for weeks at a time during the summer and fall to hunt elk and deer. Bows and arrows were the weapons of choice for hunting. Men also used boomerang-shaped clubs, which they used on small animals such as rabbits. Spears, knives, and other cutting tools were essential to the southwestern hunter.

Men from a few of the northern pueblos, such as Taos, occasionally ventured into the Great Plains to hunt buffalo. Archaeologists know this because they sometimes find buffalo bones at precontact village sites. Some tribes, such as the Walapai, relied more on hunting than on farming, since the land where they lived was poor for cultivating crops. They hunted deer, mountain sheep, and rabbits. One European document describes how the Piro kept flocks of turkeys in pens that would hold up to 100 birds at a time. They used the birds for meat and for their feathers. When drought parched the land, many tribes relied on grasshoppers and other desert insects for food.

One of the biggest hunts of the season was the communal rabbit hunt. Men, women, and children from the village participated, and the day of the hunt was greeted with excitement. After a likely site was chosen, everyone in the village formed a huge circle. They slowly closed the circle, beating the bushes and brush for rabbits and driving them into the middle. Once the rabbits were corralled inside, men and boys shot them with arrows. Rabbits were used as food and provided soft fur for warm winter blankets. In the summer, the blankets doubled as soft mattresses for sleeping.

Food was never easy to come by in the Southwest. But a thousand years of experience and an intimate understanding of the land gave the people the knowledge they needed not only to survive but to thrive on what the desert provided.

SOCIETY

Like most of the North American cultures before contact, the Southwest peoples recognized females as having the dominant lineage. The family was the most important social unit. Women owned the land, the homes, and the property of a family. Men were responsible for building the homes, hunting, making weapons, and cultivating the family's cropland. Women gathered food, prepared meals, and made objects that were needed to prepare and store foods. Both men and women were responsible for raising the children and training them to someday take on their adult roles.

Each pueblo was politically separate from the rest, even though members of the same tribe might live in different pueblos. Every pueblo had a council that loosely governed the town,

This painted bowl, found near the lower Colorado River, is decorated with three figures that may represent deities that eventually developed into the katchinas of some Southwest religions. *(The Field Museum, Chicago, Neg #A 98069)*

ISHI

In 1908, a surveying party exploring a remote area of the Sierra Nevada in California stumbled on a hidden camp. They found equipment and supplies, but everything—baskets, weapons, and tools—were entirely handmade by American Indians. The thoughtless men took everything they found, and the place was forgotten.

Three years later, in 1911, a single, starving man was found by a corral at a ranch in the hills. He had blackened his face and burnt the ends of his hair to show he was in mourning. He was taken to the local jail, where A. L. Kroeber and Edward Sapir, anthropologists from the University of California, found him. Sapir tried communicating with the man, using words from every California Indian language he could think of. When he tried a word or two in Yana, the man came to life.

He was of the Yahi tribe, a small group of hunter-gatherers that lived in the dry foothills of the Sierra Nevada. When the area was settled in the late 1800s, the Yahi were all but destroyed. Amazingly enough, a tiny group managed to survive into the 20th century. This man was the last of his band. Until his camp was destroyed, he had no idea that another world existed beyond the tangled chaparral of the mountain foothills.

For lack of a better place, they moved the man into the museum at Berkeley, where he eventually became strong enough

and the leaders of the different religious groups made up the council. Among the Hopi, one member of the council served as a chief of sorts, who dealt with the outside. There was usually also a war chief who determined when the village would go to war and with whom.

In a Zuni pueblo, each family lived in a single house of many connecting rooms. If daughters in a family got married, their husbands came to live in their home, and rooms were added to accommodate the new couples. As many as 25 people could live in one house, including a woman and her husband, all their daughters, their grandchildren, and any unmarried sons and to work as a janitor. Sapir found people who spoke variations of Yana and was finally able to communicate with the man, whom they called Ishi, which means simply "man" in Yana.

Through Ishi, Sapir and Kroeber were transported back to prehistoric American Indian life. Ishi made cords and ropes from weeds and grasses by twisting the fibers against his thigh. He made bows from juniper trees and arrows from hazel. He chipped razor-sharp arrow points in minutes and taught students how to make weapons, nets, hooks, and hundreds of other things. Ishi taught them the ceremony and ritual that went with the creation of each object—the songs, stories, and traditions of a life that had vanished years before.

He died of tuberculosis in 1916, taking with him the knowledge and experience of thousands of years. No one ever knew what Ishi's real name was. A person in Yahi society was forbidden to speak his or her own name. Everyone who had known Ishi's name was dead, and he could never be made to say it.

Most of the time, scientists must rely on silent artifacts and dusty records to tell them about life before the Europeans. In the early 20th century, however, the past became alive and taught them much about precontact life. Although this story is about a person who lived in California, the knowledge he brought to light about life long ago is similar to that of many Southeast groups.

brothers. Husbands considered their real homes to be in the households of their mothers and sisters, where they helped raise their nieces and nephews and held respected places in the family.

Zuni oral tradition describes what happened when a Zuni child was born. Both grandmothers helped. The mother's mother assisted with the birth; then the father's mother gently bathed the baby in warm yucca-root suds. She rubbed wood ash on the child to purify it, then laid the baby beside its mother on a bed of warm sand. A perfect ear of corn—the symbol of life—was placed beside the child.

In the Navajo society, marriages were arranged by the young man's father and the young woman's family, particularly her maternal uncle. If a match was made, the man's family gave a gift to the woman's family. A newly married couple got a hogan of its own, usually built next to the woman's family. A Navajo groom had to be very careful with his new in-laws, however. Strict rules made it taboo for a Navajo man to speak to his mother-in-law, meet her face-to-face, or be in the same room with her.

EUROPEAN CONTACT

The Spanish made their first expedition into the Southwest in 1539, when Friar Marcos de Niza led a party into what is now New Mexico. The promising reports he sent persuaded the Spanish government in Mexico to send Francisco de Coronado to the area the next year. Coronado's mission: to find the legendary Seven Cities of Gold, reputed to lie somewhere in the vast deserts of the Southwest. And if he came back with Native American slaves, so much the better.

His expedition was enormous: more than 300 Spaniards, approximately 1,000 American Indian guides and workers, 1,500 horses and mules, and large herds of cattle and sheep to feed the men on their journey. This large army cut through the Southwest, stripping the countryside and consuming vital water.

He stopped at almost every pueblo village he saw. At first, some of the people greeted his expedition with friendship, but they soon realized that Coronado was interested only in wealth and conquest. The Zuni attacked him as he reached the Zuni pueblo of Hawikuh, but they were defeated. The tribal leaders, knowing what Coronado wanted, convinced him there were larger cities to the northeast and northwest. Coronado, in his greed for wealth, moved on.

Coronado's effect on the peoples of the Southwest changed the course of history in North America. Horses escaped from the Spaniards and were adopted by the American Indians. In just a few years, the horse had completely transformed Native life in the Southwest.

The Apache, who until then had been farmers, quickly embraced the horse and became nomads and warriors of the Plains. Other tribes acquired horses, and in less than 100 years the horse had influenced almost every culture in the Southwest, the Great Plains, and beyond. When Europeans began pushing into the Plains and the Southwest in earnest 300 years later, they never imagined that the horses ridden by the Plains peoples were a legacy from their own past.

NOTES

p. 85   "Their village architecture . . ." Quoted in Alvin M. Josephy Jr., ed., *America in 1492* (New York: Vintage Books, 1991), p. 107.

pp. 86–88 "The precise time of arrival . . ." Robert F. Spencer, *The Native Americans: Ethnology and Background of the North American Indians* (New York: Harper & Row, 1977), p. 295.

p. 90   "The pile stick hogan has a foundation . . ." Spencer, p. 299.

p. 92   "Before the arrival of the Spanish . . ." Spencer, p. 272.

pp.92–93 "The village was up on a rock . . ." Hernando de Alvarado, quoted in Velma Garcia-Mason, *Handbook of the North American Indians* (Washington, D.C.: Smithsonian Institution, 1983), vol. 9, p. 455.

p. 93   "Five or six women together . . ." Quoted in Herbert Eugene Bolton, *Spanish Exploration in the Southwest 1542–1706: Original Narratives of Early American History* (New York: Charles Scribner and Sons, 1930), p. 177.

p. 94   "They have fields of maize . . ." Quoted in Bolton, p. 178.

p. 95   "Each one has in his field . . ." Quoted in Bolton, p. 178.

THE SALMON HUNTERS

PEOPLE OF THE NORTHWEST COAST

The winter of 1969 had settled in Neah Bay, a Washington coast reservation of the Makah, when the first odd reports came. People walking along the coastline near Ozette village noticed strange objects—pieces of basketry and planking—washing out onto the beach. The Makah tribal elders decided to investigate. To their amazement, the reports were true. They quickly called Dr. Richard Daugherty, an archaeologist who had done some work near Ozette village two years before. He took one look at the objects and knew right away, just as the Makah elders did, that something extraordinary lay buried under the wet clay above Ozette beach.

Thus began a unique collaboration between archaeologists and an American Indian tribe to preserve one of the most remarkable archaeological finds of this century: the remains of a section of Ozette village that had been destroyed by a springtime mud slide around 1450. Like a latter-day Pompeii,[*] this site still held all the trappings of daily life before Europeans arrived. Some objects stood in doorways, beside beds, and on front steps, just where they had lain when the first wave of mud flowed down the mountainside and destroyed everything in its path.

---

[*] An ancient Roman city destroyed by a volcano.

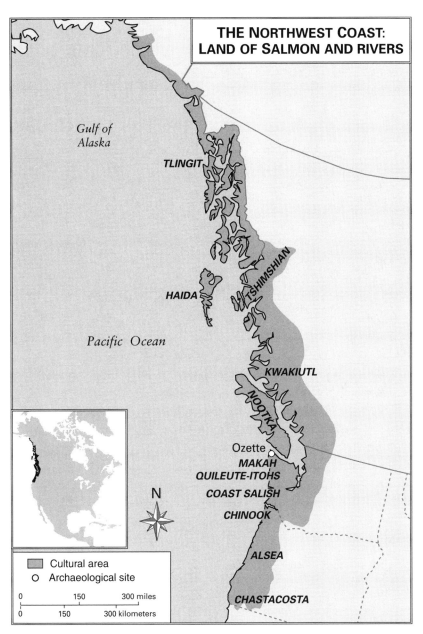

THE NORTHWEST COAST: LAND OF SALMON AND RIVERS

Gulf of Alaska

TLINGIT

HAIDA

TSHIMSHIAN

Pacific Ocean

KWAKIUTL

NOOTKA

Ozette

MAKAH

QUILEUTE-ITOHS

COAST SALISH

N

CHINOOK

ALSEA

CHASTACOSTA

Cultural area
O Archaeological site

| 0 | 150 | 300 miles |
| 0 | 150 | 300 kilometers |

The Northwest was one of the last areas in North America to see the prying eyes of Europeans. Because of this, the culture and traditions of many Northwest coast tribes remain as they were hundreds of years ago—without the influence of European intruders.

Ozette is a "wet site," which means that all the artifacts have been preserved in an area that never dried out. In Ozette, this wet area was a few feet of sticky gray mud. This wet clay kept out oxygen, which destroys objects made of wood, plants, and fibers. So these artifacts didn't rot away, which is extremely rare for objects that old. Most archaeologists never see things like this, and the site gave them a rare glimpse into the daily lives of the people who inhabited Ozette before the coming of the Europeans.

The find at Ozette was just as precious to the Makah tribe as it was to the archaeologists, but for many other reasons. These houses once belonged to their ancestors, people whose songs and stories are still told at Makah potlatches and celebrations. The objects inside the houses were—and are today—part of their history and culture. Objects that the Makah elders remember their grandparents describing were found, linking the past to the present. Each item, no matter how small, brought new depth and understanding both to the Makah and to the archaeologists who were part of the excavation.

Ozette village doesn't show the whole picture of life on the Northwest coast. The dozens of villages and thousands of people who made their homes here each had their own customs, beliefs, ceremonies, and lifestyles, some vastly different from others. But in many ways they were very much the same. They all had highly organized cultures, access to an abundance of food, and rich art styles that set them apart from any other group of Native Americans in North America.

LAND

Neah Bay, where Ozette is located, is part of a chain of mountains, coastline, and islands that stretches from the redwoods of the northern coast of California all the way to Yakutat Bay in Alaska. This stretch of land is tied to the sea and hemmed in by the coastal-range mountains along the eastern boundaries. In some places, this strip of land is no wider than 200 miles; compared with the thousands of miles of land of the Great Plains, it seems small indeed.

Rain gear was essential to the people of the Northwest coast. This man must have been well-to-do because he wears a fur robe and a woven hat. Poorer people had to make do with woven cedar-bark capes to keep dry. *(Yale Collection of Western Americana, Beinecke Rare Book and Manuscript Library)*

North of Neah Bay, in Alaska, the mountains are steep and craggy. They rise almost from the sea itself, forming wet cliffs along the shore. Farther south, the mountains rise from green pine forests to peaks crusted with ice. High in the mountains, massive glaciers feed the hundreds of streams that cascade into the coastal areas below. "In winter at the higher elevations heavy snowfalls nourished glaciers and snowfields, which in turn fed the numerous coastal rivers," quotes Alvin M. Josephy Jr. in *America in 1492.*

Throughout the Northwest coast, summers are cool and winters are wet and mild, contributing to the factors that make this area unsuitable for farming. The spine of mountains to the east traps the moisture that blows in from the Pacific. This makes the whole area damp with light rain, fog, and mist throughout most of the year. This, in turn, creates dense forests that, in some places, are all but unpassable. This moderate year-round weather creates an ideal habitat for a wide variety of plants and animals, which the Northwest coast peoples used for food, clothing, medicine, and shelter.

All these circumstances of nature combined to provide the Northwest coast people with everything they needed for a comfortable, even rich, existence. As Gordon Willey of Harvard's Peabody Museum once wrote, "There are few places in the world where land and sea combine to offer such a rich and regular bounty for human consumption, and the Indians of the Northwest Coast . . . exploited it to the full."

PEOPLE

In every culture in the Northwest, people built their lives around the sea. In the northernmost areas, the Tlingit, Haida, and Tsimshian peoples made their homes along the rugged coast and offshore islands. These people were the most isolated Northwest coast tribes. Their arts and social lives were expecially rich, and they built their houses and totem poles bigger than those of their southern neighbors.

The Kwakiutl lived in modern-day British Columbia and northern Vancouver Island in Canada. The Nootka made their homes on the western part of Vancouver Island. The Makah and the Quileute-Hoh lived along the Washington coast. As quoted in Alvin M. Josephy's book, *America in 1492,* "These people were the great sea mammal hunters of the Northwest Coast, pursuing whales and fur seals in the open ocean, harpooning them, and bringing them back to their villages to be butchered and have their blubber rendered into oil."

The southern people didn't have the resources that the northern groups enjoyed. Their cultures reflected the fact that they had to work differently to get food. These tribes, including the Chinook and Alsean, relied heavily on plant gathering and on game such as deer and elk.

According to Erna Gunther's book, *Indian Life on the Northwest Coast of North America,* most of the Northwest peoples were "well made, with even, rosy faces. . . . They had long hair, and some men wore beards." During the summer, most people became very dark-skinned from spending much time in the sun and also from painting their faces with red ocher, a dye made from plants. Some people painted half their faces, drawing a line from ear to ear across the bridge of the nose with a twig dipped in paint and filling in the upper half of the face with color. Sometimes, during ceremonies, the Nootka tossed sparkling sand on their faces, which stuck to the red ocher.

Northwest coast people wore many different kinds of clothes, depending on where they lived and what season it was. Some early explorers were amazed to see that in the summer, many Chinook men wore nothing at all. Women wore skirts made of cedar bark or silk-grass (a long, lustrous flexible fiber used for textiles) strips that hung to the knees. In cold weather, many people wore cloaks of sea-otter skins sewn together. Some people, especially women, wore capes made of shredded and spun cedar bark that was twisted into strands and woven. Along with this cape, they wore skins. Anthropologist A. L. Krober wrote the following description in a handbook for the Bureau of American Ethnology.

> The women's dress consists of a buckskin apron about one foot wide, its length slit into fringes . . . . From the rear a much broader apron or skirt was brought around to overlap the front piece. This rear apron was also fringed but had considerable area of unslit skin as well. In cold weather a blanket of two deerskins sewed together was worn over the shoulders. These capes were

seldom squared off for they liked the ragged effect of the neck and legs of the animal. The women's aprons were always made of dressed hide with the hair removed.

Bracelets, earrings, and nose rings were common with most Northwest coast peoples. Early explorers noted that both women and men pierced their ears around the entire edge. They wrote of people tying shells or knots of string in the holes for decoration. People who could afford them wore nose rings made of shiny copper or cut out of abalone shell. Some people wore feathers or quills in their noses as well. Many bracelets were made out of copper, but some were carved from shell or mountain-sheep horn. Some people wore anklets, believing that the tighter they were, the smaller the foot would be. Almost everyone went barefoot throughout the year.

In the northern areas, many women wore labrets, or lip plugs, made of shell or bone as jewelry. During a girl's puberty ceremony, her lip or chin was pierced and a small ornament, like a small plug, was inserted into the hole. As the girl grew, larger labrets were put into place. After a few years, she could wear labrets that were a few inches in diameter. For the Tlingit, labrets were reserved for the highest-ranking women of the group, but in other tribes such as the Haida, almost every woman wore one. The size of a woman's labret indicated her rank in the clan and the number of children she'd given birth to.

Throughout the Northwest coast, no one went without a hat. Everyone—men, women, and children—wore conical hats, woven in intricate designs or sometimes painted with pictures of whale hunts. At the Ozette site, archaeologists found 500-year-old hats preserved in the wet mud. Archaeologist Dr. Jeff Mauger recalls, "We found different kinds of hats. Some were flat-topped, a common person's hat. Some had an onion-shaped knob at the top of a conical hat. This would be a high-ranking person's hat. We found a whole range of hats." These hats were not only considered stylish but also shed rain and moisture in the winter and shielded eyes from the glare of water in the summer.

This Tlingit warrior is prepared for combat, clad in cedar-slat armor and wearing a beautifully carved helmet. The dagger at his waist was probably made from either traded metal or hardwood. *(Yale Collection of Western Americana, Beinecke Rare Book and Manuscript Library)*

VILLAGES

The life of each person who lived on the Northwest coast depended on two things: the sea and the forest. Villages of massive wooden houses lined the chilly, windswept beaches, and almost every home faced the sea.

Village locations were chosen to take advantage of both the ocean and the forest. Dr. Mauger observes, "There were lots of reasons why Ozette was built where it was. There's a beach with a rocky reef in front of it that's exposed at low tide. The village is situated there specifically because you don't get the heavy surf over the reef that you do farther north or south. To the southwest is Ozette Island, which blocks prevailing winds and winter storms."

Some villages were built near rivers or streams, enabling the people to harvest the massive salmon runs that occurred during the year. Most villages also had easy access to hunting areas, plenty of fresh water, wild fruits and plants, and good timber for building. People usually spent their winters there, hunting and fishing when the weather was good.

In most Northwest coast villages, the front door of every home faced the beach or water. Most villages consisted of houses built in rows, one behind the other. In some cases, the higher-ranking members of the village lived in the houses in the front row; lower-ranking people and slaves lived behind them. Some villages were built on a low bank, with a set of shallow steps that led up to the houses. The banks were not made of dirt or sand but of piles of shells, animal bones, driftwood, and rocks that had accumulated over centuries of daily life.

Based on what the archaeologists found at Ozette, they believe that the beach in front of the village was crowded with fish-drying racks and canoes, some protected under shelters made of mats. When the wind was right, the scent from the garbage piles behind the houses wafted along the beach. Scattered along the beach might have been huge whale bones and the carcasses of butchered seals, picked clean by seagulls and the village dogs.

Some villages had a graveyard either behind the village or at the end of a row of houses. In southern Tlingit villages, tall totem poles stood in front of the houses. Scattered around the village were other buildings: smokehouses used for curing fish, storage buildings built on poles, pits lined with planks for storing food and objects, huts used for steam baths, and small buildings used by women during menstruation and when they gave birth.

Most Northwest coast houses were sturdy, beautiful buildings made entirely of red cedar. Cedar is especially suited for the climate, because it doesn't mold or rot. Archaeologists found dozens of cedar planks and house beams at Ozette. The houses were rectangular structures that paralleled the beach, and each had a low, pointed roof. The walls were built of cedar planks that overlapped to keep rain and moisture from coming

TOTEM POLES

The people of the Northwest coast are famous for their enormous, intricately carved totem poles, made from cedar trunks. Totem poles could be anywhere from 10 feet to 80 feet tall, filled with images of animals, mythological beings, and sea creatures.

Totem poles are more than beautiful works of art. They served many purposes for the clan who carved it. Some were visual family trees, telling the story of the family through images of its clan animal. Others told folktales. Some commemorated an important event in a family's history or honored a respected member of the clan. These poles were sometimes built as entrances to houses; others might be used as roof supports inside. Some were placed on the graves of important people as tombstones.

Early missionaries thought these totems were worshiped by the people and destroyed many of them, usually the largest and most impressive ones. But the art and skill of carving totems was not lost; poles are still made by members of the Haida, Kwakiutl, and Tlingit tribes.

inside. On the roof, heavy rocks and huge whale vertebrae were laid on the cedar roof planks to keep them from blowing away in a storm. Some houses had cedar shingled roofs as well.

Each tribe had its own building style and way of life. In Tlingit villages, as many as 50 people might live in one house. Inside, the floor was dug up in the center and planked over, forming a shallow depression where everyone gathered to eat and to work. Encircling this area was a series of wooden platforms that rose like wide bleachers. Everyone slept on the platforms, with the highest-ranking member of the family sleeping on the top. The sleeping areas were separated from one another by wooden screens, woven mats, or stacks of wooden boxes filled with personal belongings. During celebrations and ceremonies, the platforms would be dismantled and stored. In some houses, a small trapdoor near the fire led down into a cellarlike room below, where the family took steam baths.

The large wooden interior beams of the house were usually carved and painted with images of the family's lineage—animals, figures from mythology, and religious icons. They are described in Erna Gunther's book: "At the end of the house crossbeams are supported by two carved upright posts. Each has a large human face with the mouth rounded as though the figure were calling into the distance. The post on the right has a smaller face carved beneath the mouth, and the other has a horizontal band at his waist through which about a dozen arrows are drawn. The people called the figures *ackweeks*."

Outside Haida homes, a huge totem pole—sometimes as tall as 50 feet—stood against the front of the house. Sometimes the bottom figure on the totem pole was cut out and carved to form the doorway to the house, so people might enter the home through the stomach or mouth. Inside, the homes were similar to Tlingit houses, with wooden tiers where family members slept.

The houses of the Makah were built differently but were no less impressive. Makah oral history describes houses that were built with a permanent framework that might be up to 60 feet long, 30 feet wide, and 15 feet tall. The framework was made of parallel

Inside this Nootka home, food is being prepared in a wooden box. Sleeping couches line the walls. In the rear, elaborately carved support posts stand guard. *(Photo courtesy of the Newberry Library, Chicago)*

pairs of poles. Cedar planks slid between these poles, making plank walls. In the spring, the families simply unlashed the planks, slid them out of the framework, and carried them to the summer camp. There, they'd slip the planks into another house frame for their summer home.

A flat plank roof was built on top. The roofs of the houses doubled as places where families laid their catch out to dry. Dr. Jeff Mauger explains, "If a squall or a rain came up, then people would be up passing the fish down through the roof boards. They'd move a plank and pass the fish down so they wouldn't get wet."

Drawings and woodcuts made by early explorers show that everything a family needed was stacked, hung, packed, or strewn around most homes. Carved wooden boxes were filled with clothing, woven blankets, and jewelry. If the owner of the house was a whale hunter, the walls might be hung with harpoons, nets, clubs, and baskets filled with harpoon points. Carvings of wolves, whales, seals, and birds and painted panels showing hunting scenes were also hung on the walls. Near one end of the house, a loom might be set up. Women wove blankets and fabric from the hair of dogs, mountain sheep, and other animals. Hanging from sticks along the roof beams might be hundreds of dried fish, cured and ready for the cooking pot.

In summer, most families left their villages for the fishing and hunting camps scattered throughout the islands and inlets of the coast. But the towns were never completely deserted. Those that were too old, too young, or too sick to travel usually stayed behind, spending their days gathering plants and berries and fishing off the beach.

FOOD

In the Northwest, food was so plentiful that one village could collect and store a year's worth in a single summer. The oceans were filled with salmon, trout, whales, seals, and shellfish. The forests teemed with elk, deer, bears, raccoons, and mountain goats. Freshwater fish and waterfowl, as well as otters, beavers, and other small mammals, were hunted along the lakes and marshes.

Fish dominated the diet of most Northwest coast people. In the spring, most families headed for their summer fishing villages, usually located near large streams or rivers. They relied heavily on salmon, and they spent their summers catching and preserving enough fish to last the winter. Every family and clan had its own fishing and hunting grounds, and claims to a particular spot were handed down in a family for generations. Other sites were common property, and anyone could use them.

When the camp was set up and everyone settled in, the work began. Men built rectangular fish traps made of wooden slats and set these inside a V-shaped weir with the point facing upstream. Sometimes an entire stream would be fenced in. In late summer, when water ran low, men set rows of sharp stakes across streams. Jumping salmon impaled themselves on the sticks and could be gathered later. Fish were also netted with large dip nets made with a wooden framework stretched with fiber netting.

Once the fish were caught, the women took over. Some of the catch was eaten fresh, and the women either boiled it in wooden boxes, baked it in earth ovens, or roasted it on spits above the campfire. They preserved the rest of it by drying it in the sun or slowly smoking it over a fire. Fish heads were boiled to render the grease, which was skimmed off the top and put in bladders for storage. Candlefish were especially prized. Too oily to eat, they could be lit and burned like candles. Each woman was responsible for her families' fish, and she marked her fish with special cuts to identify which belonged to her.

During the summer, while the men fished and hunted, women and slaves gathered blueberries, strawberries, elderberries, and cranberries by the bucketful. The berries were slow-cooked over a fire until they could be formed into cakes and dried. To preserve them without cooking, people stored them in containers full of grease.

Some tribes didn't have to wait for summer to hunt a prized animal. In spring, fur seals migrated in huge numbers up the coast of Washington. One of their feeding grounds, Umatilla Reef, was only three miles from Ozette village, and the Makah took advantage of it. They hunted the seals in large wooden canoes that held three or four men. The sealer carried a harpoon and a pair of inflated bladders to use as floats when he hit a seal or to keep the canoe afloat in bad weather.

Different foods had different values to the people of the Northwest coast. The foods that were the most precious were those that were the hardest to get. For example, certain fish from a specific, hard-to-access area were especially prized. Berries or roots that grew only at certain times of the year were also valuable. Some of these foods were prestigious enough to be presented as gifts for special occasions or served at feasts to show off wealth and power.

People never took the bounty of the land for granted. Hunting and fishing meant more than just a way to get food. Northwest coast people honored the spirits of the animals they hunted, for they believed that every creature had a soul. No animal was killed without a reason, and no part of an animal was wasted. They performed rituals of thanksgiving for the first fish caught and celebrated a good hunt with prayer and song.

SOCIETY

In other parts of America, long before European contact, trade, migration, and warfare enabled many Native peoples to have contact with one another. Customs were adopted, art styles were borrowed and changed, and beliefs were sifted through different cultures. But the Northwest coast was isolated from all this movement and change. Although in some ways its cultures are similar to those of other groups, many of the beliefs and traditions give it a cultural style that is, even today, distinctive.

One belief unique to the groups of the Northwest was that every child was a reincarnation of a deceased relative on the mother's side of the family. But like other cultures, they generally preferred girls to boys, because families were traced through the female line. When a pregnant woman was ready to give birth, she went to a small bark hut near her house. She and the baby lived there for ten days, assisted by her husband's sisters.

When a boy was seven or eight, he went to live with his mother's brother, who was responsible for raising him. He taught the boy to hunt and fish and instructed him in all the ceremonies and rituals that went along with these activities. Girls stayed with their mothers, learning how to prepare food, weave, and gather berries and roots.

A girl's first menstruation was celebrated by the entire clan. In many Northwest tribes, some girls were confined for as much as two years. The higher-ranked she was, the longer she stayed in seclusion. Sometimes the girl lived in the dark cellars underneath the house platforms, preparing for entry into adulthood. Her father's sister instructed her in proper behavior and clan traditions, and she fasted and ate certain foods to ensure that she would become a proud and strong woman. At the end of her confinement, the clan gave a potlatch—another uniquely Northwestern tradition—to show that she was ready for marriage. The girl was bathed and given gifts, and her labret hole was pierced or enlarged.

Most marriages were arranged between families, and it wasn't uncommon for two people to be engaged when they were small children. If the couple was older, the young woman's parents formally met with the young man's maternal uncle to propose marriage. Once a marriage was agreed on, the families exchanged elaborate gifts of property and a feast was given in honor of the couple. Most couples went to live in the woman's father's house, but sometimes a high-ranking man would build his own home for his new bride. A poor man might have to work for his new father-in-law to pay the bride-price for his wife.

Unlike other North American groups, the Northwest clans considered political rank very important. Chiefs were the heads of their clans, and their immediate family had the most power. More distant relatives were considered commoners, with much fewer rights than the chief and his family had. Usually, the members of one family, or clan, lived in one house. When a family became too large to live under one roof, some members might break away and form a "daughter house."

The biggest difference between the Northwest culture and other groups in North America was the fact that power came through the right of ownership. Clans possessed the rights to game, fish, plants, timber, water, trade routes, house sites in a winter village, summer hunting grounds, and all objects inside their homes. The chiefs had the power to give and take away a favorite fishing site, tell a kinsman when and where to hunt, and even order someone to death.

But more important, clans and individuals owned the rights to songs, stories, and traditions handed down to them by their ancestors. "This was one of the ways in which wealth was measured, by the stories, songs, ceremonies, and dances to which you had a right," says Dr. Jeff Mauger. "And these could all be traced back and transferred from one generation to the next. For someone to sing a particular song, wear a mask, or dance that dance, they have to have a ceremonial right to it."

EUROPEAN CONTACT

The first European who was sighted by the Northwest coast peoples was Captain Vitus Bering. In 1741 Peter the Great of Russia commanded him to lead an expedition to a land the

SPIRIT OF THE PESTILENCE

In 1905, a historian named John Swanson heard a legend, which might be an account of Englishman George Dixon's voyage down the Northwest coast in 1789.

All the people who moved from Skidegate Inlet to Teka'ak were dead and their children growing old, when the first ship appeared. When it came in sight, they thought it was the spirit of the "Pestilence," and dancing on shore, they waved their palms toward the newcomers to turn back. When the white people landed, they sent down to them their old men, who had only a few years to live, anyhow, expecting them to fall dead; but, when the new arrivals began buying their furs, the younger ones went down, too, trading for axes and iron.

Russians called "Bolshaya Zemblya." Bering and his crew sailed up and down the Northwest coast. They saw many people along the shore, probably the Tlingit who lived in the northern coastal areas. But they rarely came in personal contact with the people who lived in the area.

Still, the Northwest coast peoples had had some indirect contact with outsiders long before the Russian expedition—and not with Europeans. When Europeans finally arrived on the northern Pacific coast in the early 1800s, they were puzzled by the iron tools that some people had. When they asked where the iron had come from, the people explained that it "grew" in logs they had found on the beach. Years later, archaeologists realized that the Northwest coast peoples had been salvaging iron spikes and hardware from the remains of Japanese vessels shipwrecked at sea. Some of these iron artifacts are found at dig sites today.

Other than this indirect contact with the Japanese and an occasional European ship sailing along the shore, the Northwest coast people were left pretty much alone. It wasn't until the mid-1800s, when the opening of the Oregon Trail brought thousands of whites to their lands, that they began to be seriously affected by European expansion. Even then, most of them withstood the impact of contact, keeping much of their heritage and culture intact.

NOTES

p. 106   "In winter at the higher elevations . . ." Quoted in Alvin M. Josephy Jr., *America in 1492* (New York: Vintage Books, 1991), p. 51.

p. 106   "There are few places in the world . . ." Gordon Willey, quoted in Philip Kopper, *The Smithsonian Book of North American Indians Before the Coming of the Europeans* (Washington, D.C.: Smithsonian Books, 1986), p. 201.

pp. 106–7 "These people were the great sea mammal hunters . . ." Quoted in Josephy, p. 52.

p. 107   "well made, with even, rosy faces . . ." Quoted in Erna Gunther, *Indian Life on the Northwest Coast of North America As Seen by the Early Explorers and Fur Traders During the Last Decades of the Eighteenth Century* (Chicago: University of Chicago Press, 1972), p. 9.

pp. 107–8 "The women's dress consists of a buckskin apron . . ." A. L. Kroeber, *Handbook of the Indians of California*, Bureau of American Ethnology, #78, 1924, reprinted 1953, p. 76.

p. 108   "We found different kinds of hats . . ." Dr. Jeff Mauger, archaeologist, Makah Cultural Research Center, Neah Bay, Washington, interview by Allison Lassieur (April 1997).

p. 110   "There were lots of reasons why Ozette . . ." Mauger, interview (April 1997).

p. 112   "At the end of the house . . ." Quoted in Gunther, p. 27.

p 113   "If a squall or a rain came up . . ." Mauger, interview (April 1997).

p. 117   "This was one of the ways . . ." Mauger, interview (April 1997).

p. 118   "All the people who moved . . ." Quoted in Gunther, p. 121.

7 IN THE LAND OF SNOW AND ICE

PEOPLE OF THE ARCTIC AND SUBARCTIC

There is fear in the longing for loneliness
When gathered with friends and longing to be alone.
Iyaiya-yaya!
There is joy in feeling the summer come to the great world,
And watching the sun
Follow its ancient way.
Iyaiya-yaya!
There is fear in feeling the winter come to the great world
And watching the moon now half-moon, now full
Follow its ancient way.
Iyaiya-yaya!
Where is all this tending?
I wish I were far to the eastward, and yet
I shall never again meet with my kinsman.
Iyaiya-yaya!

—ancient Inuit spirit song

In a remote area on the northern slope of Alaska stands a small house. Or, rather, the remains of a house. All that's left now are some chips of wood, a few willow branches tied together, and piled blocks of sod. This house looks as if it has been here for centuries, built by precontact Arctic peoples who lived here

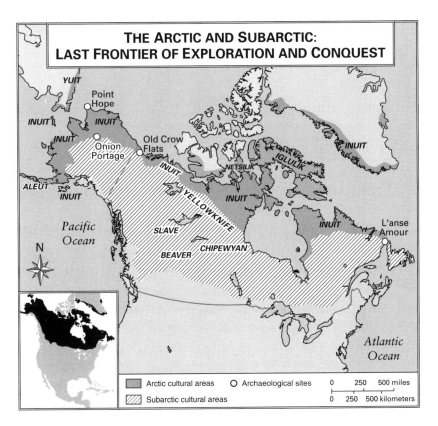

THE ARCTIC AND SUBARCTIC: LAST FRONTIER OF EXPLORATION AND CONQUEST

Although a few explorers sailed up the northern coast, few ventured into the Arctic and Subarctic until well into the 19th century. Even today, most of the Native Americans who still dwell here live the way their ancestors did before the coming of the Europeans. These people all called themselves Inuit—Europeans added the locations to the names for their own convenience.

hundreds of years ago. Its shape is that of an ancient house, a form that the northern peoples used as they traveled the frozen, treeless plains of the Arctic tundra in search of caribou and reindeer. It is made with materials that were easily available. Inside, under a few inches of dirt, is the final clue to how old this house really is: a rusty coffee can from 1910.

Archaeologists who found this house quickly realized that it was built only 70 or 80 years ago. They could also see, however, that it told a much older story. The person who lived in this house was a bridge between past and present. Although this person was from a recent time, he or she knew how to build a home in the middle of nowhere in the style of his or her ancestors. He or she probably had relatives who were alive when the first Europeans ventured into that area of Alaska in the early 19th century. And this person—like Native Americans throughout North America—most likely carried the history, stories, and songs of the people who lived on the land hundreds of years before.

LAND

The Arctic is an enormous area that sweeps more than 4,000 miles from the northern coast of Siberia across Canada to the eastern shores of Greenland. This land, with its miles of tundra and its cold, treeless coasts, is as inhospitable as it looks. The lack of trees makes the wind especially bitter, bringing with it the frigid air from even farther north. During the winter, darkness descends on the land for months. Summer is the time of 24-hour days, when the sun never sets. In summer, the temperatures fall below zero, and winter brings temperatures of 40 below. It is so cold that bare skin freezes almost instantly.

Subarctic people of Alaska and the Canadian islands inhabited a land far more hospitable than that of the people of the Arctic north. This area covers everything from the interior of Alaska to the Labrador Peninsula across what is now Canada. This vast region has many different habitats, from conifer forests that stretch unbroken for millions of miles to mountains, prairies, and hundreds of lakes and rivers. Although the Subarctic climate isn't as harsh as is that of the Arctic, bitterly cold winters can still last seven or eight months. In the northern tundra areas, the ground is frozen for most of the year. In the summer, the sun melts the ground and turns the tundra into vast, soggy wetlands. Lakes and rivers became natural highways; people traveled by canoe in spring and with snowshoes and sleds in winter.

The people living in the Arctic and Subarctic had to deal with many of the same problems: extreme weather, isolation, and the constant struggle for food. However, the distinctive areas in which they lived made their ways of life different from one another. Each group responded to the challenges of its environment, and each one developed a society within the restrictions put on it by the natural world.

PEOPLE

The Arctic was home to a number of groups, whom many people called "Eskimos." According to archaeologist Ken Shoenberg, "None of the Arctic people called themselves that; their name for themselves is Inuit, which means human. 'Eskimo' was the insult that the Athabaskins [a nearby group] used to describe them. The word means 'eaters of raw flesh.'" Another group, the Aleut, are closely related to the Inuit, and their precontact ancestors also made their home in the Arctic areas. The Inuit were not organized into tribes but instead banded together in families and became known by the areas where they lived.

The people of the Subarctic were known as the Athapascan because they all spoke a similar language. They, too, were organized into bands, which were larger and more loosely related to one another than were their Arctic neighbors. These bands included groups with colorful names such as Slave, Beaver, Chipewyan, and Yellowknife. They followed great herds of caribou, moose, and reindeer in spring and summer, then trekked to lakes and beaches to fish and hunt seals in winter.

A key to successful living in the Arctic and Subarctic was wearing the right clothing for the weather. Each group adapted its clothing for the environment it lived in. Explorers in the 1800s described the basic wardrobe of most groups, which consisted of garments made of heavy skins and fur. Styles differed from place to place. The Aleut wore long, bulky coatlike outer garments made of fur or bird skins. Inuit coats had hoods lined with fur, and women's hoods were pointed. Skilled hunters kept their families well clothed in richly decorated coats made of the best caribou hides. It was a sign of prosperity when a family could replace its clothes every year. Poorer families had to make do with wearing clothes longer or using sealskins instead.

In the Subarctic, where it was warmer, people usually had two sets of clothing, one for winter and one for summer. The two sets of clothes looked similar: a long dress or shirt with a hood and long sleeves. The only difference was in how many layers people put on. Both men and women wore two or three winter garments, usually made from elk or caribou skins, for warmth. In summer, people wore only one caribou skin coat. Caribou calf–skin leggings and thick, knee-length fur moccasins protected legs and kept feet warm. Some men and women wore fur mittens with a string that looped around the neck.

Inuit women of the Arctic usually wore their long, black hair in braids that were rolled and knotted in two buns in front of their ears. Sometimes they carried their sewing equipment in their hair rolls. Men also liked wearing their hair long, usually to the shoulders and tied away from the face with a band. In the Subarctic, men wore their hair short, in a bowl-shaped cut above their ears. The younger boys had their long hair tied back with thongs of sinew; when they entered adulthood (usually after their first kill during a hunt), they cut their hair short.

Some of the older men, the most respected hunters and fishermen, wore round bone lip plugs, called labrets, in holes at the corners of their mouths. Others had blue-black lines tattooed along their mouths, cheeks, and shoulders. Women also had tattoos on their faces, arms, and breasts. They made their tattoos by coating a sinew thread with an oil-and-soot mixture, then using a needle to run it through the skin.

VILLAGES

The first image that comes to mind when people think of Arctic houses is an igloo. Somehow, it became a common belief that all northern peoples built and lived in these round domes of snow throughout most of the year. The reality is that people rarely, if ever, lived in igloos.

Homes had to be easy to build because the northern people moved constantly. In summer, groups followed the herds of elk, caribou, and other animals as they searched for pastureland. After a successful hunt, people froze the meat on the spot by burying it. They would then return to that spot and build their winter villages there.

In winter, many of the Arctic peoples set up camp along the frozen coastlines, near massive herds of seals and walrus, and spent their time hunting. In the interiors of the Subarctic, winter camps were located to take advantage of good hunting and fishing grounds. Housing had to built with the materials at hand, and it had to be warm—no matter what the season.

The Athapascan peoples of the Subarctic lived in many different kinds of houses, depending on what materials were available. Archaeologists and historians rely on written evidence to reconstruct the homes. A good all-weather home was the conical lodge made of bent poles and covered with bark (summer) or hides (winter). This kind of house could hold many families and, in winter, could be easily heated with one fire. Other families built large wigwams, round structures made from poles dug into the ground and bent over to form a dome. These were tied together at the top and then covered with bark, hides, or branches. Wigwams usually were summer homes, since poles couldn't be thrust into the frozen ground during winter.

A third kind of house looked much like a tipi from the Great Plains. Many large poles were set in a circle, leaned inward, and tied to a center pole. This cone-shaped frame was then covered with skins or bark. In summer, hunters and travelers sometimes built temporary lean-tos of branches and bark. These bark-and-wood structures were warm and comfortable inside. People covered the dirt floor with fir branches, then, according to the *Handbook of the North American Indians*, published by the Smithsonian Institution, laid down "mats, or sealskins as soft as velvet; upon this they stretch themselves around the fire with their heads

OFFERINGS TO THE
ANIMAL SPIRITS

Hunters of the late precontact Arctic made beautiful weapons that depicted both real and imaginary animals. The Inuit believed this beauty pleased the animals' *inuas*—their spirits. An animal that was killed with honor returned to the body of another animal to repopulate the earth.

Carved ivory arrow straightener: This carved ivory animal, perhaps a caribou calf, was used to straighten wooden arrows. It's only a few inches long, but someone took the time to delicately carve its folded legs, round eyes and ears, and even its tiny mouth. *(Field Museum, Chicago, Neg. #A 103543)*

The Inuit became known for the beauty of their carved tools. No implement was too small or unimportant to be adorned. Tiny ivory fish lures were carved with fins, gills, and ribs. Jumping fish decorated bone fishhooks. Elaborately carved animals swirled along harpoon shafts and knife handles. Even tools for fixing tools were not overlooked. Carvings like these brought beauty to every hunter's home and invited the animal spirits to be generous to his family.

resting upon their baggage. And, what no one would believe, they are very warm in there around that little fire, even in the greatest rigors of the winter."

People of the frigid Arctic coasts needed houses that were simple to build and easy to heat. Pacific coast Inuit built their winter villages beneath embankments, sheltered from the biting Arctic wind. Summer fishing villages were located at the mouth of a good salmon stream. Villages weren't large, only a few houses, but several families lived in each home. There could be up to 200 people in one village.

Their rectangular houses were built of sod and branches, whale bones, and sometimes drift logs foraged from the beaches. Insulating moss and lichen grew in the sod, keeping the insides of the houses warm on even the harshest winter night. Inside was a common area in the center of the house where families gathered for meals, to work on projects, and to pass the time. Around the sides of the house, separated by curtains of skins, were small cubicles where people slept.

Hunters of the Arctic built smaller, dome-shaped, semiunderground houses of sod, driftwood, and whale ribs. A long entrance tunnel angled downward to the living quarters of the house, which was usually a foot or two beneath the ground. Shelves in this tunnel held food, gear, clothing, and other personal objects. In the living area, sleeping benches ran around the walls. In some houses, the doorway was in the roof, and in others there was an opening in the roof, covered by translucent gut to let in light. The floor was covered with fur and branches, and a single lamp kept the entire home cozy in all kinds of weather.

Because frozen objects don't rot, archaeologists have been lucky enough to find many things left behind by the Arctic peoples, including entire houses. Ken Shoenberg explains, "We have frozen wood; we have organic remains in some places. You can tell whether the people living in the house were sea mammal hunters, because we sometimes find soil that is still saturated with grease, oil, or fat. Many of the old houses were built with whale bone. A whale jawbone makes a good doorway."

FOOD

At first glance, many areas of the Arctic and Subarctic look empty of all life. Could any creatures possibly live in such a desolate place?

The answer is yes, quite a few. Although the lands looked barren, they teemed with reindeer, caribou, bears and polar bears, mammoths, oxen, and moose. The sea provided whales, seals, walrus, and sea

These Greenland Inuit move in for the kill during a whale hunt. Their umiaks, made of walrus skins stretched over wooden frames, could hold up to 50 hunters. *(Photo courtesy of the Newberry Library, Chicago)*

lions. Shellfish lived in the shallows, salmon and cod filled the offshore waters, and seabirds by the millions returned each spring to mate. Even the sparse brush and lichen of the tundra was home to voles and lemmings—mice-sized rodents that provided food to anyone able to catch them or to find their seed-filled nests.

The people of the Arctic and Subarctic were meat eaters almost exclusively. No crops could grow in the harsh, cold environments, even in the more southern areas of the Subarctic. The men hunted and fished, and women gathered the wild berries and plants that did grow during the cool, short summer months.

The Subarctic Athapascan and Algonquian were big-game hunters, following the herds of caribou and moose throughout most of the year. During summer and winter migrations, groups of hunters built huge enclosures, sometimes up to a mile around, of branches and stones. When a herd was sighted, some hunters drove the animals into the enclosure while others killed them with arrows and spears. A favorite way of hunting was to spear the animals as they crossed rivers and lakes. The hunters, two to a canoe, speared an animal in the kidney with a long, lightweight lance tipped with a bone or an antler point.

In the southern areas of Canada near the St. Lawrence River, people hunted and trapped a huge variety of animals, such as beavers, porcupines, foxes, hare, woodchucks, and squirrels. Waterbirds made good eating, and the lakes and rivers were filled with eels, trout, salmon, sturgeons, and smelts. Women gathered raspberries, blueberries, strawberries, cherries, wild grapes, and wild apples. Most food was smoked or dried and stored for winter.

The Inuit and the Aleut of the Arctic coasts were big-game hunters as well—but they hunted the game of the sea: seals, sea lions, sea otters, walrus, and all kinds of whales. They also fished for salmon, halibut, codfish, clams, shrimps, crabs, and octopuses. Seabirds were snared, and hunters collected their eggs by either climbing a cliff to the nests or being lowered from the top. An early European explorer wrote that "they gather among the crags a great quantity of eggs, with which the ships that arrive supply themselves."

SEAL HUNTING

One of the first reliable written accounts of life in the Arctic came from Hans Egede, an early missionary who lived in western Greenland for fifteen years. In 1736, he published a book about Inuit life, which included the drawing on page 131 of how Inuit hunters captured seals.

His drawings bring to life the ways of the seal hunter. Looking at them, one can see that seal hunting required teamwork and cooperation. Hunters first explored areas of ice-covered ocean, marking the location of each seal breathing hole. Because seals used many breathing holes, no one could predict which hole would be used at any time. Each hunter stationed himself at a hole and waited, motionless.

The wait could last for hours. Some seal hunters sat next to their breathing holes. Others watched seals as they clambered onto the ice, then let their harpoons fly. At large seal gathering places, groups of hunters circled the hole and stood poised, ready for the seals to surface. Sometimes the hunters worked in pairs, one standing between a seal and its breathing hole as the other stood ready. This teamwork continued after the hunt was over. When the hunters brought their game back to the village, the wives of successful hunters butchered the animals, dividing them into parts and giving specific pieces to families whose hunters weren't as lucky. If a hunter came back empty-handed, he could rely on other hunters to provide his family with food.

Although the people had plenty of food, the most important food animal was also the biggest and most dangerous to hunt—the whale. The whale was more important for the Arctic cultures than for any other. The defining part of Arctic life was the whale hunt. Taking a whale was a difficult, life-threatening job, and the whale hunters of the north did not take it lightly. Before a hunt, the owner of the umiak (a long, open boat made of walrus

Western Greenland Inuit used a variety of techniques during a seal hunt: stalking a seal, sitting beside a breathing hole, and surrounding an opening in the ice to harpoon animals there. *(Photo courtesy of the Newberry Library)*

skin stretched on a wooden frame) made sure that each hunter had new clothes, that all the lines and equipment were new, and that prayers and songs had been offered for a successful hunt. While the umiak was at sea, the hunters stayed silent as the harpooner—one hunter chosen for his skill and strength—sang songs and chants to entice the animal to the surface.

European explorers who witnessed a whale hunt reported that when a whale was sighted, the crew paddled as close as it could. Then the harpooner threw his weapon into the side of the enormous animal. The harpoon was designed so that the shaft fell away and left the point, held by lines of hide, buried deep in the whale's skin. The lines were attached to floats made of inflated sealskins, which dragged on the wounded animal as it tried to escape. Each time the whale surfaced, the harpooner let another shaft fly. The hunters might follow the animal for hours, until the exhausted whale finally stopped.

Hunters then jumped from the boat onto the back of the whale, weapons in hand. Some men cut the sinews of the whale's fluke to keep it from swimming away. Others stabbed the head, lungs, kidneys, and heart. As the whale bled to death, other umiaks filled with hunters paddled to the animal, and they all towed it to the edge of the ice.

Then it was time to celebrate. The wife of the boat owner greeted the returning hunters with songs and prayers, and the entire village turned out to help butcher the animal. The meat was divided among all the families, and piles of blubber and skin were set aside for the crew members. Some of the meat was cooked and eaten on the spot, but the rest of it—as much as six tons—was stored in caches. Men dug pits and lined them with stones. Then the meat was put in. The cold weather froze the meat. One whale could keep a small village supplied with food for almost a year.

The Arctic people understood the ties between the land and themselves. For them, hunting was more than a way to provide food and shelter for their families. Animals were part of creation, joined to one another and to humans by trust and understanding. They respected the game as they respected themselves, knowing that without the animals, they would die.

SOCIETY

The isolation of life in the Arctic and Subarctic defined the cultures of the people who lived there. Most of the time, small bands of related families lived together in tiny enclaves of a few houses. At certain times of the year, during large hunts, or in areas of good hunting, people would come together in larger villages and enjoy the companionship of others for a few months. For the Inuit, freedom was very important. Families were free to leave one group and join another through marriage or friendship.

Most people stuck together in small hunting bands of a few families. Each house might be home to two or three related families, such as a father, his sons, and their families. Unlike the matrilineal societies of other American Indian groups, the Subarctic and Arctic cultures recognized kinship on both sides of the family. There were no chiefs or organized governments in the cold wilderness; people made decisions by discussion and consensus. Leaders usually were in charge of organizing things rather than controlling them. Life was too hard to quibble about politics, and everyone shared the resources so all could live.

Special houses were built for women, where they went when they were menstruating and to give birth. They stayed there for a few days after a baby was born, helped out by other women in the family. Families welcomed the births of girls and boys with equal happiness, for neither was more important to the lives of the group than the other. For the first two years of their lives, children lived in a skin bag lined with moss or rabbit fur. Sometimes children were dipped in cold water outdoors to stop them from crying.

As they grew, boys and girls were taught different skills. Boys learned how to hunt and make weapons, and all the rituals and songs surrounding these tasks. Because good hunting skills were so important to survival, a boy's first kill was cause for great celebration by the entire band. No matter how small the game was, it was cooked and shared by all the hunters. Girls learned from their mothers how to cook, sew, and tan animal skins for clothing.

Marriage was very simple for most people in the Arctic and Subarctic. Two people who cared for one another began living together, and they were recognized by the rest of the group as a couple. Among the Aleut of the Arctic, a man interested in marriage had to work for his future father-in-law for a period of time. After this bride service was complete, the couple were married. They usually lived with the wife's family until a baby was born, then moved into the husband's family's home.

Women's work and men's work were of equal value in the family. Stable marriage was vital to survival in the Arctic and Subarctic. Among the Inuit, if a family had only girls or boys, it was common for it to adopt a child of the other sex to balance things out. The children were usually orphans from within the tribe. In this way, the family was assured that the band would survive. The children were raised as members of their new family, learning the family's songs and ceremonies.

EUROPEAN CONTACT

By the time Europeans "discovered" the northern peoples of the Arctic in the early 18th century, the Aleut and Inuit had at their command a vast store of knowledge and skill. They knew the land and the animals as well as they knew one another. They had sophisticated weapons, a rich culture, and spiritual beliefs that tied them to the land and had enabled them to live for thousands of years in the frozen north.

The first Europeans who ventured into the Arctic were Russians, who came to the Arctic coasts in search of furs. They didn't build permanent homes but instead sailed over to hunt and trade with the Inuit and Aleut of the coastal areas. These early encounters had little impact on the people at first; many bands never saw the few Russian traders.

The Polar Inuit, the northernmost American Indian group in North America, didn't see their first European until 1818. Until the moment when Scottish explorer John Ross landed in their homeland in northwestern Greenland, they thought they were the only people in the world.

Other Europeans, especially the French, penetrated the interior Subarctic areas. One of the first Frenchmen to enter Canada was Jacques Cartier, who sailed up the St. Lawrence River in the 1530s. Fur traders and explorers were on his heels, ready to make their fortunes trading furs. Most of the American Indians, however, lived in difficult-to-get-to areas that few Europeans cared to colonize. Only the groups who lived in southern Canada and along the Atlantic coast were immediately affected by the Europeans, who quickly decimated them with warfare and disease.

In 1670, the Hudson's Bay Company of Great Britain began building trading posts along the shores of Hudson Bay in northern Canada. By the 1800s, a vast network of trade routes, river traffic, and trading posts cut through the Subarctic from the Atlantic to the Pacific, supplying even the most remote Subarctic groups with European goods.

But even with the arrival of whites, the northern societies that had endured for thousands of years changed little. Trappers, explorers, and missionaries who braved the climate rarely ventured far from established forts and towns, leaving the native peoples to themselves. Today, the trappings of 20th-century life—television, computers, and other modern conveniences—have come to even the most remote parts of the area. But most native people still respect and live by the knowledge and culture of their ancestors. Their traditions, songs, and stories survive.

NOTES

p. 120   "There is fear . . ." Quoted in Alvin M. Josephy Jr., ed., *America in 1492* (New York: Vintage Books, 1991), p. 27.

p. 123   "None of the Arctic people . . ." Ken Shoenberg, archaeologist, National Park Service, Anchorage, Alaska, interview by Allison Lassieur (May 1997).

pp. 125–26 "mats, or sealskins as soft as velvet . . ." Edward S. Rogers and Eleanor Leacock, *Handbook of the North American Indians:*

The Subarctic (Washington, D.C.: Smithsonian Press, 1981), vol. 6, p. 175.

p. 127   "We have frozen wood . . ." Ken Shoenberg, interview (May 1997).

p. 129   "they gather among the crags . . ." Quoted in Margaret Lantis, *Handbook of the North American Indians: The Arctic* (Washington, D.C.: Smithsonian Press, 1984), vol. 5, p. 175.

EPILOGUE

▲

THE STORM BEGINS

There are moments in history about which one can look back and say, "At that moment, the world changed forever." One of those moments is the early morning of October 12, 1492, when a cannon aboard the *Pinta* fired, signaling the sight of land. The Europeans who came to the New World after this cannon shot brought a storm of change to the people who were already there. As the trickle of explorers, traders, colonists, missionaries, and adventurers became a flood, their contact with the American Indians had results that no one had dreamed of.

In Florida, contact threw many of the native tribes into chaos as the Spanish killed and destroyed their way through the land. Missions sprung up where villages once stood. People were forced into slavery to harvest crops for the Europeans from the very fields they'd once cultivated as their own. Others were pressed into hard labor, building homes and towns for the Spanish. Weakened from disease and starvation, they died by the thousands. Replacing all this slave labor became a problem for the Spanish, who began to travel north into what are now Georgia and Alabama to capture more people. When the new native slaves began dying too fast to be replaced, the Spanish began importing black slaves from the coast of Africa—the first to come to America.

In the Northeast, the effects of contact penetrated the area much faster than the Europeans themselves did. It transformed American Indian politics, social structures, and intertribal relations. People died from disease by the thousands. Some tribes were wiped out in a few days. For those who were left, the European hunger for furs set tribes against one another, creating bitter enemies and strong alliances between groups who wanted the European riches that the fur trade could bring them.

Farming communities began spending all their time collecting furs for Europeans. Others stopped hunting big game such as deer and moose for food and hunted smaller animals such as beavers and foxes. Women, whose jobs were tending crops and preparing hides, spent more time with the skins than they did in the fields. Soon, this imbalance forced American Indians to trade their furs for food to feed their families. Gradually, many tribes became dependent on the Europeans for most of their food and belongings and began losing the knowledge and skills needed to live on their own.

The fur trade also had a huge impact on the Great Plains, but in an indirect way. As some northeastern tribes became stronger through trade, they pushed westward, conquering weaker tribes and taking over their lands. These tribes moved farther west themselves, settling on the fringes of the Great Plains in farming communities and nomadic bands. When the horse arrived, some of these tribes—who were once peaceful farmers along the Atlantic coast—became the stereotypical hunters of the Great Plains.

The arrival of the horse in North America is second only to Columbus in the impact it had on American Indian life. Less than 100 years after the first escaped Spanish horses came into Native hands, the horse was an indispensable part of life to most Great Plains and Southwest tribes. Tribes who once lived together in uneasy peace could now attack and decimate their enemies with greater speed and power. The only way for other tribes to keep up was to acquire horses themselves. People who had lived for generations in one place could now travel to other lands, building villages and lifestyles far removed from what they had once been. European disease also followed the horse, claiming thousands of people and forcing weakened Southwest tribes to abandon their once great adobe cities.

For the people of the Northwest coast, European contact meant only one thing: disease. Although some tribes didn't see their first European until well into the 19th century, it didn't take long for European sicknesses such as smallpox, cholera, and others to wipe out entire tribes. This wholesale death had a deep impact on the culture of the Northwest coast. People in this area measured wealth not by material possessions but by the songs, stories, and dances a person had a right to. Diseases killed whole families, and their songs and stories were lost or "stolen" by other families. Even today, 200 years later, ownership of some ceremonies is controversial.

Most Europeans did not *intend* to wipe out Native Americans. While most wanted to rule them, take their land, or change their culture, few really wanted them all dead. And despite European contact, American Indians survived. Some of their traditions have changed because of European contact; others were created to take the place of things that were destroyed. But the American Indians' continued existence in 20th-century society, so different from the societies their ancestors knew, is proof of the strength of their culture, which no one could destroy.

ARCHAEOLOGICAL AND NATIVE AMERICAN SITES ON THE INTERNET

▲

ArchNet (http://www.lib.uconn.edu/ArchNet/)

A good place to start; includes thousands of links to Native American sites on the Web. ArchNet lists archaeological organizations, parks, historical sites, universities, and museums that deal with the archaeology of American Indians.

Cahokia Mounds (http://medicine.wustl.edu/~mckinney/cahokia/cahokia.html)

One of the most impressive precontact mound cities, Cahokia is the home to Monk's Mound—bigger at its base than the Great Pyramid in Egypt. This site tells the history of the Cahokia Mounds and includes the archaeological dig record and a map of the park.

History of the Cherokee (http://pages.tca.net/martikw/)

This site chronicles the history of the Cherokee people, from before European contact to today. Maps, photos, records, charts, and links to other Cherokee sites.

National Park Service (http://www.nps.gov)

The Links to the Past area of the NPS Web site has wonderful graphics, photos, and links to parks throughout the country. Ancient sites and historic places are also covered.

Native American Navigator (http://www.ilt.columbia.edu/K12/naha/nacurr.html)

This site serves as a clearinghouse for information on the Web on Native Americans in North America.

NativeWeb (http://www.nativeweb.org)

This is a very useful site to go to for information about American Indian tribes today. It includes history, museums, photos, reports, news, parks, organizations, events, and links to current Native American organizations.

North Carolina Archaeology (http://www.arch.dcr.state.nc.us)

Another good jumping-off place for links to Native American sites. Includes archaeological sites in North Carolina, a history of the Cherokee people, information on other groups that lived in the area, and links to museums with Native American holdings.

South Dakota Archaeological Research Center (http://www.sdsmt.edu/wwwsarc/)

For archaeology of the Great Plains, this is a good site to visit. Includes photos of artifacts, excavation information, and research information on digs around the country.

State of Florida/Bureau of Archaeological Research (http://www.dos.state.fl.us/dhr/bar/arch.html)

This site is full of graphics, photos, artifact images, and links to archaeological sites on the Web. A kids' area has pictures, tours, facts, and information about early Florida American Indians.

Tennessee Archaeology (http//www.mtsu.edu/~kesmith/TNARCHNET/ArchLinks.html)

This site includes a list of web sites on archaeology to visit.

SELECTED
FURTHER
READING LIST

▲

NONFICTION

Griffin-Pierce, Trudy. *The Encyclopedia of Native America.* New York: Viking Penguin, 1995. A young-reader journey through precontact Native America.

Johansen, Bruce, and Grinde, Donald. *The Encyclopedia of Native American Biography.* New York: Henry Holt, 1997. Six hundred life stories of important people in American Indian history, from contact times to the present.

Josephy, Alvin M., Jr., ed. *America in 1492: The World of the Indian Peoples Before the Arrival of Columbus.* New York: Vintage Books, 1991. A fascinating series of essays on life before the arrival of Columbus.

Kopper, Philip. *The Smithsonian Book of North American Indians Before the Coming of the Europeans.* Washington, D.C.: Smithsonian Books, 1986. A region-by-region journey through American Indian history, this book focuses on how archaeologists work and what they look for during an excavation.

Thomas, David Hurst. *Exploring Ancient Native America: An Archaeological Guide.* New York: Macmillan, 1994. An adventurous account of some of the most important American Indian archaeological sites in North America. Includes a comprehensive state-by-state listing of parks, museums, and historical organizations that have American Indian holdings.

Viola, Herman J. *North American Indians.* New York: Crown Publishers, 1996. A book for younger readers, this volume traces the history of many precontact tribes. Also included are first-person stories from Native Americans living today.

FICTION

Dorris, Michael. *Morning Girl.* New York: Hyperion, 1992. Morning Girl is a member of the Taino—the first native people Columbus encountered—living with her family in the Bahamas in 1492. She and her brother, Star Boy, tell of life in their sunny world before the "visitors" came.

———. *Sees Behind Trees.* New York: Hyperion, 1997. This is the story of Walnut, a nearsighted Native American boy living in 16th-century Virginia. His eyesight keeps him from mastering many skills, including shooting a bow and arrow, that will prove he's an adult and entitled to a new name. His uncle invents a new contest to "see what can't be seen," and Walnut must use his other senses to succeed and earn his adult name.

O'Dell, Scott. *Sing Down the Moon.* New York: Bantam Doubleday Dell, 1973. Fourteen-year-old Bright Morning is captured by Spanish invaders of her canyon home.

Preble, Donna. *Yamino Kwiti.* Berkeley, Calif.: Heyday Books, 1940. Long before the whites come to California, Yamino dreams of becoming a messenger. He longs for the freedom and adventure of running from village to village. But the tribal elders want him to become a priest instead.

Sewall, Marcia. *People of Breaking Day.* New York: Simon & Schuster Children's, 1990. In this lavishly illustrated picture book, the Wampanoag people of southern Massachusetts describe themselves and their beliefs during the time of Massasoit—right before the first European contact.

Vick, Helen Hughes. *Walker of Time.* Boulder, Colo.: Robert Reinhard, 1993. Two Hopi Indian boys, Walker Talayesva and Tag, travel back in time 800 years to their ancesceral cliff-dwelling home. Walker, a contemporary Hopi, and Tag, the son of an archaeologist, learn about the ancient culture of the Sinagua people and try to help with the problems that could destroy their cliff homes—and their culture.

INDEX

▲

Italic page numbers indicate illustrations.
Boldface page numbers indicate major treatment.

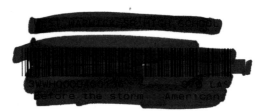